G000160974

CHARLES REES

LIFE AND DECLINE OF THE FAMILY DOCTOR

authorHOUSE®

AuthorHouse™ UK
1663 Liberty Drive
Bloomington, IN 47403 USA
www.authorhouse.co.uk
Phone: UK TFN: 0800 0148641 (Toll Free inside the UK)
*   UK Local: 02036 956322 (+44 20 3695 6322 from outside the UK)*

© 2021 Charles Rees. All rights reserved.

No part of this book may be reproduced, stored in a retrieval system, or transmitted by any means without the written permission of the author.

Published by AuthorHouse 12/17/2020

ISBN: 978-1-6655-8357-2 (sc)
ISBN: 978-1-6655-8358-9 (hc)
ISBN: 978-1-6655-8360-2 (e)

Print information available on the last page.

Any people depicted in stock imagery provided by Getty Images are models, and such images are being used for illustrative purposes only. Certain stock imagery © Getty Images.

This book is printed on acid-free paper.

Because of the dynamic nature of the Internet, any web addresses or links contained in this book may have changed since publication and may no longer be valid. The views expressed in this work are solely those of the author and do not necessarily reflect the views of the publisher, and the publisher hereby disclaims any responsibility for them.

CONTENTS

INTRODUCTION

In 1954, I was taken to the East Cliff at Bournemouth, where I was born and had lived, to see the Battleship Vanguard. It was our last battleship, and the potential power of its 15" guns was colossal. Had it wanted to, it could have destroyed Bournemouth, Poole, Christchurch and possibly, most of Southampton too without shifting position. I was fascinated by the 20th century Royal Naval history, and the advent of the dreadnought and the subsequent dreadnoughts were very much a part of this. I did not realise at that moment that I was looking at the last of our dreadnoughts. The age of the dreadnought battleship had come and gone in the space of fifty years, two generations, and made obsolete by advances in warfare.

When I eventually settled for a career as a family doctor in the National Health Service (NHS), I had no idea that the concept of a family doctor in a group practice would also become obsolete ten years after I retired. The general practitioner (GP) survives, granted, but it is very different from the creature of my day. I realised that there would never be a family doctor who held a personal list of 2000 to 2500 patients for thirty-eight years as I had. There may have been a few but not anymore. I had kept meticulous records of events – always analysing, reflecting and looking for ways to do things differently. I still have the yearbooks – thirty-eight of them – with records of every home visit. I still have a DDA record with every event worthy of requiring strong drugs and the reason thereby. It has a detailed report on the changes in that period. It recorded the epidemics, whooping cough in 1977, Type A influenza in December 1989 and others. I realise that this may be a unique record from the days of family doctors because since my retirement nearly ten years ago from the Practice, much has changed.

After retiring from the Practice, I worked as a locum in six Practices for over seven years. It was a wonderful experience because I was able to work just for pleasure without any responsibilities. However, I did not realise that during that time, the age of the full-time family doctor was fading, and the age of the 'portfolio' doctor was ascending. These doctors, of both genders, worked for just a few sessions a week in GP and supplemented their work with something else. With time on their hands, they were able to become dominant in these areas. There is much to be said for this, but there is the issue that they ended up doing very little general practice and doing much of jobs they were not trained for. A GP is a 'jack of all trades and master of none.' No problem there. In fact, medicine needs at least one generalist. But unfortunately, the best way to learn as much as possible from the huge gamut of medical presentations is to see more patients. The new GPs see fewer patients and, exhausted by the plethora of presentations, decide that the solution would be to drop a session. The correct solution would have been to see more patients, not less.

Of course, family doctors still exist, but they are aware that they are a dying breed. They carry on with a pervading air of despair. This book is not alluding to a golden age because there never was one. The world was very different then, and I would like to record it and the fascinating patients who affected my life. The generation of doctors I had worked with had gone through WW2. They worked hard throughout the day but often played golf in the afternoon. They largely did not reflect on things but did it because that was the way they were done. In the spectrum of being good and being nice, they tended to be good. It is of merit to be both, of course, but the modern doctor has to be nice rather than good. The weight of persistently being nice to all, however odious, rude or downright aggressive they might be, is very wearisome. There is no outlet. And though being good is virtuous, it is no longer enough. It is now more important to follow guidelines however wrong they may seem. But one size never fits all. The guidelines are very useful to young doctors, especially if they have little experience, but they are framed by people who have read medical papers and not by doctors who have seen patients. So, while the old doctors wanted to be good, though they weren't always nice, the new doctors are nice and follow guidelines.

So, what is the difference between a GP and a family doctor? General practitioners came into existence with the NHS Act of 1947 and started working in 1948. Strictly speaking, a GP is a self-employed doctor who is sub-contracting mainly, but not entirely, to the NHS. This gives the GP some special privileges concerning pensions in particular. Their duty was to fulfil the terms and conditions of service, and naturally, there were always some right at the beginning who simply did this and no more. But most followed the tradition of being constant and loyal to their patients, which meant going beyond the terms and conditions when appropriate. In my lifetime, there were some outstanding role models, such as John Frye from Beckenham in Kent. He started his practice in 1943 and, believing there were few effective treatments, jotted down something about every patient he saw. Nowadays, almost all the existing diseases and conditions have been altered by treatment, and so, the natural history of common illnesses is not known. But thanks to John Frye, it was. He liked to quote WHO's definition of good health – "Health is a state of complete physical, mental and social well-being." He would add with a twinkle in his eye that the only time anyone felt like that was during the act of sexual intercourse!

To start with our Terms and Conditions of Service were short enough to be read, and they were negotiated between the NHS and the profession. As time went on, the Government realised that it was the more powerful partner in the arrangement and could change things at will. In 1990, a new set of Terms and Conditions appeared and the writing was on the wall. The Government wanted a population-based approach, which I will explain later, and from that moment, doctors worked for the Government and not their patients.

When I retired from my practice, I joined the local Probus. I met men who had held important jobs all over the world. Their knowledge of the world and its working was vast, but their knowledge of the human condition was not. They had been looking through a telescope of world experiences whereas I had been looking down a microscope. When I talk to them and think of my thirty-eight years in Clayford in East Dorset, I marvel at my limited ambition and horizons. And yet, at the time, it did not seem like that. Each year and each day brought forth new challenges to drive me on. The job was never done. It was like building sandcastles on the beach – every wash of the waves undid the previous build. For every condition that was cured or alleviated, the patient brought forth new problems that came with age. I still drink at the local British Legion with some old patients, mostly bricklayers. How I envied them! They could go back ten to thirty years later and still see a wall they had built. So, do I regret it?

The simple way to answer is to relate it to a story. Many years ago, I was pursuing my post-graduate education at Bath. At breakfast, I was sitting next to an interesting Doctor who worked at the Rheumatology centre there. Without prompting, he suddenly dived into a recitation on his glittering career: He had done this and that, received many awards, held a professorship in California and was now a consultant at Bath. People had stopped talking, and there was a listening silence. The room went quiet. And then, for some reason, I started with my response. When I was eleven, I said, my mother died, and in the years that followed, I decided I hated illness and death. I wanted to do something about it and by fifteen, I had made up my mind to be a doctor. I went to medical school at eighteen and was qualified at twenty-three. When I entered general practice, all I wanted to do was to be a family doctor. I wanted to bring people into this world and ease them out of it when the time came. I wanted to diagnose measles, mumps, chickenpox and all the usual illnesses that plague peoples' lives and help them to cope with them. That is what I have done, and it has been a privilege. There was an even heavier silence in the room. I had never meant to put my consultant friend down, but he most certainly had been. Most of the doctors there were just like me with similar stories. There were doctors for whom family medicine was a passion and a privilege and not just an academic exercise. I think that answers the question. That answer and the truth behind it kept me going for forty-eight years and offering help to 300,000 patients in the NHS!

A FAMILY DOCTOR

I HAVE ALLUDED TO THE DIFFERENCES between a GP who fulfils their Terms and Conditions of service and a family doctor. I could explain this in detail by offering a huge number of examples, but here are a few.

I was very lucky because the doctor I replaced had been in Clayford for about forty years, except for six years at the war. Thus, there were a large number of middle-aged to elderly patients who had only ever known two doctors – Ian and myself. He told me many tales that proved to be invaluable as time went on. One of the older characters was Bert. He was a pointer by trade, which was a well-paid but boring occupation. Bert used to talk as a coping strategy. He could keep talking and would always be interesting. He claimed he had never had a day off in his life, which was probably true, in one respect, matched by the fact that he had never done a full day's work in his life! One day, after he had genuinely retired, he had come to me looking unusually glum. I asked him what the problem was, and he mentioned the name of one of his daughters. She had been diagnosed with Huntington's! Huntington's chorea is caused by an autosomal dominant gene; it appears in middle age and results in premature dementia and death. It is awful and could affect fifty percent of any offspring. Bert was upset and wondered how his family of six children would take the news. Thanks to those chats with Ian, I found a way out. "Yes, but Bert, she isn't yours anyway." This information would not help the unfortunate lady, but it meant there were no implications for the rest of the family as Bert had six children but only one of them was his. I wondered if Bert knew how I knew this, but he never asked. He just looked relieved as though he had forgotten about his unfaithful wife's high sex drive and loose morals. I think the modern portfolio doctor only looks at the tip of the iceberg when they see a patient. Knowing them and their families for over decades makes such a difference.

I remember another incident involving two sisters who were very close. The elder had carcinoma in situ of the cervix, which, in those days, was treated with a cone biopsy. This was very different from the modern practice of minimal invasiveness, but it did end the issue. The younger sister had regular smears but somehow slipped through the net and went on to have invasive cancer. The progress of the disease was inexorable and awful as those who know will understand. I was involved very closely with the family– her husband and two children – throughout. When she became terminal, she and the family wanted her to be at home. One of the ideas my senior partner, Jock, had impressed on me at the outset of my work was that we need not be confined to our official hours. Visiting at night or on weekends, whenever appropriate, was alright. I knew many family doctors who visited on Sundays, almost pastorally, even when they were not on call because it was quiet. This family who had stuck together through this ordeal realised that their loved one might die in the middle of the night and have the death certified by a stranger, who would mutter condolences but who would not have known the young mother at all. When asked, I willingly gave my home phone number as it was a privilege to be asked to attend. It duly happened at about two in the morning. We chatted as I certified, and it helped them. Clinic doctors don't have this bond that, thirty years later, still exists.

Margaret was a solicitor's secretary and was about the same age as me. She was single with a son whom she brought up alone. I really knew nothing else about her background. She didn't seem to have any other family or support. She had a chronic indigestion problem and, from time to time, had gastroscopies and appropriate treatments. When she returned once with a new case of indigestion, I organised another gastroscopy. But this time, cancer of the stomach was found. She had undergone all the current treatments but with diminishing success. The time eventually came for her to be admitted to our local MacMillan unit for the last time and it was organised for midday. After the morning surgery had been completed, I felt I could not let the moment go. So, knowing she was not to be admitted until lunchtime, I dropped in to visit her. She was pleased to see me and said she would be out and back home soon. I knew it was not to be, but I didn't know if she did. What was I to say? Anything I could have said would have been complete flannel. She was going to die. How do you talk about that without being sanctimonious or lying? I had had a heck of a morning in surgery. Each patient had been an absolute so-and-so, to use our ever-so-British vernacular. Just then, I had a brainwave – I would not talk about her; I would talk about me. I told her about the morning I had had. I regaled stories of awkward patients with their petty complaints, funny beliefs and chaotic lives. We both began to laugh more with each story until I noticed her discomfort. Her abdomen was full of fluid, ascites, due to cancer, and laughing was making her uncomfortable. I stopped and became serious again. For ten minutes, I had taken her mind off herself. Patients can be very funny; they are people with all sorts of stories, and she had enjoyed listening to them. She too calmed down and then looked at me and said, "my son and I were so lucky to have you as our doctor." That is why being a family doctor is so special. I never saw her again.

Mary was a lovely woman of about sixty, who was well-spoken and well educated. She was fairly plump and, it gives me no pleasure to say this, outwardly quite unattractive. But her personality was warm and lovely, and she was clever. So, I had often wondered why she had married that overweight, coarse, bully of a husband. He was ignorant and odious. She also had very severe psoriasis at a time when treatments for it were limited. Every now and again, it would flare up dreadfully. I sought help from my predecessor, who was like a great oracle. He knew all about it; his depth of knowledge about the patients always astonished me. One often hears people saying on the radio or television that their doctors don't know things because they never inform them. But the truth is they tell us everything, and we don't always want to remember them! Ian recited the whole sad tale. For reasons unknown, this cultured lady had married this uneducated brute who bullied her as and when he wanted sex. To use Ian's exact words, *"he trussed her up like a chicken and buggered her."* He usually repeated this. She did not like it and became more stressed, which made her psoriasis worse.

Psoriasis has a genetic basis but, like a lot of skin conditions, is made worse by stress. At least I now knew what triggered it, though I was unable to do anything about it. However, one day, the hubby, who was a binman, lifted one bin too many and slipped a disc. In those days, many back conditions were treated by immobilisation in a plaster jacket. They weighed about half a stone, circumnavigated the body, and, most importantly, made sex impossible! Mary's psoriasis cleared – a miracle. We continued to talk but never about her sex life. Whatever abilities Ian had to get information out of distressed ladies was not yet available to me. However, she did reveal what a bully her husband was and how he would wait for her to come home with her pension to snatch it from her. I gave her my usual counselling concerning bullies. Most ladies, not surprisingly, are afraid of what might happen if they stand up for themselves, but most bullies are frightened of losing control over their victims and not over themselves. One day, she came in with a smidgeon of triumph on her face. She had confronted hubby and told him that from now on, she was her own woman and would take no more. "What did he say?" I asked with admiration. "He took it," she began, *"but,"* she stretched out the word, *"he doesn't like Dr Rees!"* Well, so be it. I could take that if it meant the restoration of her self-respect.

About a year later, I received a call on a Monday night, it being my night on duty. It was Mary. She said she thought her hubby had died in his chair. I shot around, and indeed, he had. We sat and talked, and I asked what had happened. He was not a healthy man with heart disease and diabetes and was well overweight. *"I made him dumplings for his dinner,"* she said, *"and he had two, which was quite enough, but he said, 'give me two more."* I told him Dr Rees would not like it! He then said, *"give me the dumplings; you can sod Dr Rees." "He ate them and then, he died!"* I was not sure whether having my name cursed in a dying breath was a good thing. One thing I did know was that she was genuinely upset at his passing. Despite everything, she had sincerely loved him. But the fact that you could cure a lady's psoriasis by putting the husband in a plaster jacket was another thing they had not told me at medical school!

Charles and his wife were in their sixties, and one winter's night, they had decided to do some late-night shopping. They got into their car and had set off onto Wimborne Road but had rammed straight into a parked car. At the moment of contact, the owner was filling his car up with petrol. He was squashed like a fly on a window. The previous evening, he had run out of petrol but had just managed to roll his car down the incline to rest it outside a local garage. He had walked home and was not able to return until the following evening when he had filled a can from the garage and had proceeded to fill the tank. At that moment Charles and his wife were on their way to do some late-night shopping. Charles was interviewed extensively by the police. He hadn't been under the influence of alcohol, his vision was good, and he was fully conscious with no known medical conditions. Moreover, he had never been in any accidents. He simply didn't see the man or the car. The man could have come and gone at any time in the past twenty-four hours – it was just one of those frightful things. Life went on, but two weeks later, something got into my head, and I knew I had to ring Charles up. I asked him if he was alright and he said he was. *"You haven't been out for two weeks, have you?"* I asked. He said he hadn't. I knew it somehow and understood it too, but this could not go on forever. So, I tried to counsel him. *Did you mean to kill the man – of course not; what did you mean to do – late night shopping. Could the night have happened differently – of course it could have if they had started earlier or later or not have happened at all or if the man had not run out of petrol or come and gone at any other time.* Thus, we went through the entire scenario. Someone else could indeed have resuscitated Charles's confidence (not his wife, who was equally traumatised) but surely, it was right and proper that the family doctor do it pro-actively.

A family doctor was also the advocate of the family at times when there seemed to be none. In this country, the final arbiter of the management of a child is the court and not the parents, which is not so in most European countries. Though the family has no rights at all, they may have strong opinions. A common example is when a young girl is pregnant with an unwanted baby. Through social services, the baby is put up for adoption. Though the parents of the girl may not want their grandchild adopted, who is their flesh and blood – their daughter's child – they have no rights. Fortunately, I had been involved in several cases where the grandparents had adopted the child as their own and all ended well. And as a family doctor, I was glad to play my part.

Though I have tried to explain the differences between being a family doctor and a GP, there is no more poignant explanation than that given by Don Berwick in his John Hunt lecture, and I make no apology for quoting it because he puts it across far more articulately than I could. He describes his father, who was a family doctor in a small rural town in Connecticut.

"*He was a person of privilege. His privilege was to enter the dark and tender places of people's lives – our people. He knew secrets. He knew – we didn't – that Mary, browsing the market shelves next to us for her cereal, had miscarried again; that Nicholas, who sold us shoes, was struggling with alcohol; that Maureen, our Club Scout leader was quietly beside herself because Jonas was depressed and using drugs. He knew that Mrs Krazinski, who taught fifth grade, had lung cancer and was going to die from it, even though she did not know because they hadn't told her yet.*" Those dark and tender parts of people's lives were what we had to live with. It was a privilege, but it took its toll.

HOW DID IT ALL START?

WHEN I WAS TEN, THE family had moved to Southport in Lancashire. My mother, who was said to have developed asthma when she was nineteen, had become ill during the second winter, presumably with a chest infection. We all took turns to be with her; there was no TV then, we just had to sit by an electric fire. Eventually, she grew worse and was admitted to a hospital. I went to stay with a saint of a lady, Mrs Murgatroyd. She was totally selfless and lived for her family, friends and anyone in need. She was an extraordinary woman. She had two sons but had had a third child, a daughter, and the girl was severely handicapped. She was told to take the baby home and turn her every two hours and she would live for a fortnight. Mrs Murgatroyd took her baby home and turned her every two hours for eighteen months before she died. She would bring me bars of white chocolate and assorted books. One book I loved was a series about a doctor who went to Tanganyika, as it then was. Occasionally, as the weeks passed, I was able to visit my mother from the garden of the hospital. Children were dirty things and not to be allowed in as they might bring infection. I stood in the garden and talked to her as she leant out of the window. The visits became fewer, and when the phone rang, Mrs Murgatroyd would answer it after closing the door. One Monday evening, my father arrived and told me that my sisters and I were going to the hospital, and Mummy was going to die. We trailed in to see her in an oxygen tent. She did not see us. The next morning, my father arrived and said she had died at 4 am that Tuesday morning.

The years that followed were difficult for the family as my sisters left home and my father remarried. His new wife had been a nurse in the Queen Alexandra's Royal Army Nursing Corps and had received the Burma Star during WW2. You had to be within a certain distance of enemy lines for two years to get it. According to her mother, she had never had any childhood infections or any of the infectious diseases she nursed, which was just about everything except Typhus. She was a frequent smoker but gave my father at least fifteen years of a quality life after his stroke. I always say it's the smoking that got her because she died when she was 97 in comparison to her mother who did not smoke and died at 101.

However, the point is that, by the time I was fifteen, I had decided I did not like illness in general and death in particular. I was determined I would do something about it; I would become a doctor. And whatever one might think about that sort of vocational slush, it made me a doctor at twenty-three and work for forty-eight years. One of my daughters had obtained a degree in Maths and had a good job in London. But she had decided it was not going to fulfil her and she changed course, gave it all up and was lucky enough to get into Hull and York Medical School. She found she had qualified on exactly the same day of the week and date of the year that my mother had died and which had made me resolute in my career. Coincidence? Probably. Spooky? Definitely.

WHY CLAYFORD?

I DID NOT WANT TO BE a GP. At medical school at Leeds, we had spent a week in general practice, and although I had not known it at the time, I had spent mine with a legend – Barry Colville. I have never seen anyone work so hard. We started at eight in the morning with surgery and visits and arrived at his house at 1 pm, ate for twenty minutes, and then we were on our way for more visits and the evening surgery, which ended at about 7 pm. I jotted down something about each patient. I found it amazing as one patient after another, who were known to him, came in with clear trust in him. My head reeled. It was stimulating, impressive and exhausting but, to a fifth-year medical student, it seemed too much like hard work!

I really wanted to be a surgeon, particularly, an accident surgeon. I loved the emergency and trauma side of orthopaedics. At that time, there was no career path in accident and emergency, which posed a problem. Also, to be a surgeon, one had to start by passing the primary FRCS examination, which was not only hard in those days but had a 95% failure rate! It was a time consuming and expensive feat. But things are easier and certainly more different now. One day, the orthopaedic surgeon I was working for announced, *"My old friend, Ian Limbery, is retiring, and they will need a replacement. You should apply!"* I had not thought about general practice and did not even want it, but this was a command and, clearly, my application was not optional. I duly attended the interview in Clayford with Ian and Jock. It was pleasant but pointless – they wanted an older man, and I did not want the job! But it was pleasant. I had done as instructed and all was well and temporarily forgotten.

A year later, things had changed as they do. My wife, a nurse, became pregnant and, thus, would be out of work soon. There was no maternity leave then. My job was also coming to an end as it was on a six-month contract. We lived in a flat in Sandbanks and needed a house. In the winter, there were cheap places to rent in Sandbanks, but that winter, there were electricity strikes, and it was not much fun to come back to a place with no electricity after a long day's work. On the political scene, Edward Heath and Anthony Barber were flooding the country with money and house prices were rising. If we were both sure to be earning, which we weren't, we could have just about afforded the average house at that time, which was about £6000. I had thought of entering general practice and had applied and been offered jobs in Lancashire, Swindon and Wolverhampton, but my wife did not want to move.

One day, as we sat in that miserable bungalow facing the abyss, the phone rang. It was the Clayford practice asking if I was still interested in the job I applied for the previous. Was I interested! When I arrived at the practice, I heard the sorry tale of what had happened in the past year. They had eventually appointed a doctor of suitable age, but he could not cope with the night calls. This, unfortunately, was not the only issue. He was Jewish. Nothing wrong with that, of course, but he allegedly – I've only heard the rumour – had an improper relationship with a nun from the Holy Cross Abbey up the road! This did not go down well in a small, closed community as Clayford was then. He had to go, and he did. This was their first disaster.

They then appointed a doctor in his mid-fifties who they thought would be more suitable to the ambience of the area. He was a disaster. He had a huge array of qualifications in the medical directory – medical, dental and an MD from Malta – but most of them had been bought. A few months after I started, a lady came to me saying she had been bleeding from her vagina. She had called the doctor at Christmas, who said she should come to the surgery when she had stopped bleeding, and then, he would examine her. She came to see me in May when, by some miracle, she had stopped for a while. I examined her, and there was a huge cavity from cancer in the uterus – appalling negligence! She was treated with radiotherapy and, thankfully, responded very well to it. The patients were afraid of him, and the staff loathed him. Jock and a soon-retiring Ian were overloaded.

And so, just when I was desperate for a job, they were also desperate for a doctor. Their two attempts at finding a suitable new doctor had been disastrous. Jock would be left with an expanding list with only 'the disaster' to help him! I could not lose! And so, I started working, but six months later, I had no security. A six-month period of consideration was quite normal and acceptable, but there was still 'the disaster' between Jock and me. So, I wrote down all the reasons Jock should offer me a partnership and recited them over and over again to myself. I then asked to see him alone. I walked in, and just as I was about to make my oration, he said, *"Oh, before you start, I've gotten rid of Dr xxx (the disaster), and I want you to become a partner."* I was speechless. I never did make my speech. I still have it – written but unspoken. Six years later, Jock retired, and I was the senior partner for the next thirty-two years!

Jock's retirement was a huge event for the practice. When I had started, the practice was run by two receptionists and a finance lady, Miss MacDonald. By the time Jock retired, the practice and our staff had more than doubled. We decided to throw a big event with a presentation and speeches, where Jock would retire and the new partner would be welcomed. Ian Limbery, who had retired when I had joined, arrived with Miss MacDonald in a car. I never knew her as anything else but Miss MacDonald. She was single and ageless. Ian Limbery had been very fit in his day but had osteoarthritis in both hips and a very early hip replacement, the Jouet. It was what is known as reverse geometry, but the problem was the metals used. They formed an electric cell and disintegrated. He would not have a revision, and so, he hobbled around on two sticks in a fair amount of pain. The patients who called out to him felt mortified when they realised that he was in a worse condition than they were. He hobbled out of his car with a cry, *"A glass of water for Miss MacDonald,"* and hobbled back in. A secretary rushed out with the water to find Miss MacDonald dead in the car. Was it Ian's driving? His car had so many dents that you would avoid parking next to him. Or was it Miss MacDonald's sense of timing? Maybe if she could not work for Jock, she would work for no one! We did not know the reason, but thirty-eight years later when I retired, some clearly remembered this incident and waited expectantly for something to happen.

Jock enjoyed his retirement until he was eighty. One Easter weekend, he was admitted to hospital with a chest infection. They told him he had pulmonary fibrosis; he said he did not. They showed him his respiratory function tests; he disputed them. He died the next day. One of his many sayings was, *"Charles, you must be 100%. It doesn't matter if you are 100% right or 100% wrong; you must be 100%."* He believed in the placebo effect due to much experience. Unfortunately, in his last case, he was 100% wrong! I missed him terribly and still do.

FIRST DAY

MY FIRST DAY AS A GP in Clayford was on April 4, 1972. The senior partner, Thomas Cecil McDougall-Morrison, asked me to see a few patients and do some visits afterwards. He was known to his friends as Jock, and after about a year, he asked me to call him Jock. I loved that man, and it was easily the happiest time of my career. Jock said many memorable things and one of them was *"Charles, the first twenty-five years are the worst!"* It was a bit of a joke, but as the decades went on, I realised how right he was.

Looking back, the world seemed so primitive. There was only one traffic light in Clayford. Only 40% of the homes had telephones. The first traffic warden did not appear until 1975. And that year inflation reached 27%. Many of the roads had not been constructed, and travellers often stayed in the woods or common land, of which there was a great deal.

The first visit of that morning was a few miles away where two children were unwell. Their mother was young, attractive and very pleasant. Over the following weeks, she came to see me, and we built a rapport. She struggled with headaches. I analysed her carefully eventually told her that I believed she was experiencing migraines but had a background of tension headaches. Tension headaches are said to be caused by muscular tension (never proved, I think) which can be due to physical or stress-related issues. I told her I could treat the migraines, and then, we could review the situation. When she returned the next time, she informed that the migraines had gone; she still had other headaches, but she was content to leave things as they were. A few weeks later, I received a message asking me to drop in if I was in the area. On one hand, I was always in the area because we did a lot of home visiting; on the other, I was aware that she was an attractive young woman who was around my age, and this was something to be cautious about. In those days, the remotest liaisons with patients were hanging offences! I decided to call in anyway and sat down as she brought a cup of tea. Then, she started talking. *"When I was seventeen,"* she began, *"I was courted by a man twice my age. He was very worldly, as I was not, and courteous and polite. He was the same to my parents, who liked him and were reassured by his business and money. We eventually got married, and after the wedding, on the first night, he took my clothes and underwear off and put them on himself. I was horrified. That is why I get headaches."* I reflected later that they never taught us this in medical school! *"But you had two children,"* I said. She admitted that she was floundering and confused, and then, her mother fell ill, so she just went along with it. She had two lovely children and, apart from the cross-dressing incidents, the marriage was a good one. But she did not like it. She then offered to show me the drawer where he kept his other underwear. I declined! I met her again, and we had several counselling sessions. I suggested she confront him. Bullies (I was not convinced he was a real bully albeit he had groomed her) hate being challenged. He was not a violent man, and so when she challenged him, he was horrified. The cross-dressing in her presence stopped and so did her headaches. I knew him socially and he was always good company. He was a builder. He smoked and drank heavily, and at age fifty-two, he had a heart attack and died. His wife and I always had an understanding. I was the only person who knew her secret and that was enough. Years later, I bumped into her while she was crossing the main road with a new husband. We looked at each other, and she was clearly very happy. As I said, they don't tell you all that in medical school!

Sometimes, the bond between a patient and their doctor is priceless. David was a tall, strong young man with whom I played football. I had joined the local football team, which brought along many long-lasting friends. David developed a non-Hodgkin lymphoma and was treated accordingly. When remission did not last, they realised it had been staged wrongly in the first place. Sadly, he died aged thirty-five.

David's mother (I never knew his father, but I believe he was a good man) was a hard woman. She looked and talked hard and had difficulty in expressing her emotions. That was probably why she had few friends, and as the years went by, they passed on as well. But she had her family doctor, who knew her son when he was in his prime. Sometimes, she would come in just to talk about David. Sometimes, she would come in just to be there. I knew that, however superficially, I was a link to her lost son, and I was happy to just sit and be.

WORST MOMENT

U NDOUBTEDLY, THE WORST EXPERIENCE IN my medical journey in
1986. A young man was brought to me by his family. He was a
very pleasant person, but his mind was a bit mixed up after travelling
to Hong Kong and beyond and taking all sorts of drugs. This was a
new era of drugs, one which neither I nor the psychiatric department
was prepared for. Drug abuse had occupied a very small part in my
work life; there were plenty of other things to attend to. I had attended
a post-graduate meeting on chemical dependency at that time, and the
psychiatrist had explained how it was overwhelming their psychiatric
work. Mental illness outside drug and alcohol abuse was peripheral, and
doctors could help by referring as few patients as possible. The NHS was
overwhelmed with work, but some occasions were worse than others.

However, a psychiatrist and I managed this man with some success
over a couple of months. His parents lived in Hong Kong and were
lovely people. His father had ankylosing spondylitis and, around this
time, had eventually succumbed to it. His mother was a lovely smiling
lady who coped with it all and the father had asked me to look after her
when he had gone.

Mondays were always bad and felt like stepping onto a rather fast
treadmill. Just after lunch, I received a call that there were two visits
with patients who had hypomania and were at opposite ends of the
practice. Knowing that there would also be a full day of surgery of
goodness knows what, my heart sank; I always liked to be running at
the same speed as the treadmill. The days were always at least ten hours
long, and after thirty to forty patients with two, maybe three, problems
each, my mind was tired and befuddled. Nevertheless, I sped off to the
first patient, whom I did not know very well. He was not taking his

medication but did not seem too bad. I retraced my steps and crossed the practice to our young man. When I arrived at the house and looked through the window, I saw him climbing over the wall at the end of the garden into the woods by the river. What was I to do? Should I have chased him? And if I caught him, what was I to do with him? I talked to his mother. She was confident he would return but had called because she thought he was deteriorating. I returned to the practice and called up the psychiatrist to ask for a domiciliary visit, which was the accepted way to deal with these situations. One psychiatrist for the whole of East Dorset was clearly not enough. The Mental Health Team had taken over this now. However, the psychiatrist was not eager to come that day. I remembered the education session previously where the psychiatrist had urged us not to press for responses; so, I just informed the psychiatrist that I needed a domiciliary visit for two patients – one who would not take his medication but I was not worried about and the other who I was worried about but would take his medication. I later rang up the mother, who confirmed that her son had returned home and taken his medication. I was always on-call on Monday nights, so I thought that if there was a problem, I would be there to deal with it.

At about 7 pm that night, the young man hallucinated that his mother was a witch and suffocated her with a pillow. The incident was not discovered until Tuesday afternoon, which was my afternoon off, so I only learned of the tragedy on Wednesday morning. As my partner who had been called on Tuesday recounted the event, he also told of his irritation at being disturbed during the surgery! It was almost surreal to listen to this horrific story from my partner who was completely oblivious to the horror of it.

Could I have done things differently? Churchill had reassuringly said, "let those people who have been in that position be the judges." Looking back through the retrospectoscope, one can always find an alternative. But, what about in reality? I think I made a written statement but was never asked to attend the inquest. Maybe doing so and making a verbal statement would have helped me, but life went on, barely missing a step. The family was very understanding. The young man was admitted to a mental hospital and, for all I know, may still be there. Normally, one would want a person to be cured and their mind restored but, in this case, to what reality would he be restored? This is what haunts me – his reality is that he had murdered his mother.

MENTAL ILLNESS

O NE OF THE MOST DIFFICULT, time-consuming and unrewarding tasks in the early days was obtaining a certification of mental illness. Now, one has to only make a phone call to Social Services or the Mental Health Team to deal with this onerous and unpleasant job. But in those days, the whole responsibility fell to the GP. First, the psychiatrist would have to be called, who may inform that sectioning under the Mental Health Act was required. Sometimes, one would have to arrange the psychiatrist as well as social workers, an ambulance and, often, the police, all at the same time. Getting these four agencies plus oneself and, of course, the patient all together at the same time was a tricky juggling act. They all had other jobs to do and were often reluctant, and you would always have another surgery waiting. And unlike delivering babies, there was never a happy ending. It was made more difficult by the fact that my senior partner, Jock, would have nothing to do with sectioning. Years ago, he had sectioned a lady when she was psychotic. Subsequently, she had recovered, and when she was better, she sued him in the courts. It must have been a very unpleasant experience as it went to the Winchester Crown Court. Anyway, he would not do it anymore, and so, more fell to the rest of us. It was the only task he was unhelpful with though as one of his favourite sayings was "if everyone does a bit, then nobody does too much." He was against doctors who cherry-picked, but not in this case.

Rarely did everything go to plan, but in one case, it went right off the rails. One Wednesday morning, one of my partners asked me if I could certify one of his patients. He had been trying to do it all week but one agency or another, including the patient, had always been absent. The psychiatrist had signed his part of the certificate, and he just needed the social workers to apprehend the patient with the help of the GP. Since Social Services knew all about it, he said it was just a formality. At lunchtime, I received a phone call from Ted Balls, an elderly social worker I had worked with before. He was highly competent, and I had a lot of time for him. I was relieved. The patient in question, a woman, lived in a flat above the shops on Ringwood Road. She had just gone out and was probably on the way to the Post Office around the corner in New Road. My time was precious as I had a huge antenatal clinic to do. So, I suggested that I drive around, park on the wide pavement in front of what is now the Chianti Italian restaurant, and wait for them to bring her to my car. Since it was a Wednesday afternoon, shops were closing early, traffic was light on the roads and there were few people about. I parked and waited, watching through the rearview mirror. I saw a lady appear; two men closed in on her and ushered her to my waiting car. She was naturally in a state. As Ted pushed her in my car, the lady remonstrated. Then, Ted asked me, *"Do you know this lady?"* Of course I did not! It was my partner's case! You could have heard a pin drop. *"Neither do I,"* said Ted, *"The case was handed to me an hour ago."* There was an icy silence as the two social workers and I realised that no one present knew the lady we were trying to section! We had apprehended the wrong lady! We had lifted a blameless human being from the roads of Clayford. And now, she was in my car. I was an accessory to kidnap!

Thankfully, she was a sport. Apologies and weak explanations were repeated, and she took it all in good faith. Ruffled but relieved, she got out and walked away. Thank heavens we had never heard of her after that. Did she relate the story to her friends? Was she famous for a while? Luckily, there were probably no witnesses to the scene.

All credit to Ted and his co-workers who had multiplied to four by now, also not cognisant of the lady in question. They were not fazed by the occasional unexpected kidnap; they wanted the job done. So, they went back around the corner and returned with another lady, angrier and feistier than the last. They dragged her into my car. *"Call the police,"* she kept shouting. I needed no prompting. I sped off the pavement onto the road, shot across to the police station a few hundred yards down and deposited them all there before wishing a rapid farewell and making a speedy return to the antenatal clinic. That was enough excitement for one afternoon. Amazingly, I never heard any more about the incident.

EPIDEMICS

A s I WRITE, THE WORLD is in the grip of the COVID-19 infection. Such a pestilence had been forecast for ages because the vast population and extensive travelling was bound to rapidly spread disease. In 2015, Bill Gates suggested we prepare for a pandemic instead of war. When HIV arrived in the 1980s, it fooled everyone because it was nothing like any known viral infection. However, it stimulated progress in the knowledge of viral infections and encouraged reflection. It alarmed the Society of Actuaries because it introduced mortality in a younger age group, which seriously upset their Life Assurance predictions. In the 1990s, they produced a paper offering five scenarios that may or may not occur. In the end, none of them came true because of the clean needle campaign. The lesson we should learn here is that even the cleverest brains can make wrong predictions because of an unknown factor. I became interested in type A influenza and the epidemic of 1918–19. It is now known as the seasonal flu, probably because every generation has to take ownership by renaming everything to the confusion of historians. Those experts who refer to the seasonal flu, however, are probably unaware that the seasonal element is in the very name. Type A influenza has the intriguing property of spreading at an inversely proportional rate to ultraviolet radiation. It occurs during winter in the Northern and Southern hemispheres. It follows a cold snap; hence, it was named *influenza di fredo* – the influence of cold. So, don't go out without your coat! In the 1990s, it occurred to me that many patients in their nineties would remember the 1918 flu and be able to tell me about it. How I wish I had recorded these interactions, but all that is left are a few stories in my head. I managed to get about a dozen candidates. Strangely, half of them remembered nothing of this terrible epidemic – nothing at all. Among the other six, four remembered it but could add little new information. One woman, Queenie, had been at school in Bournemouth and remembered that they had all been sent home, but they were not anxious because they knew they would not get it. They believed it would affect young adults but not children. Trestles and tables were taken from the school to accommodate the bodies of the victims. Maurice had been eight or nine at the time and remembered it clearly. He was aware that people had been used to death as news of it came regularly from abroad during the Great War, but they were not used to funerals. The bodies of the soldiers were the property of the War Office and were eventually buried by the Commonwealth War Grave Commission near the place where they had fallen or the hospital where they had died. Suddenly, with the 'flu epidemic, funerals were frequent happenings, and he clearly remembered the fine black horses with their black tassels pulling shiny black hearses. A prominent memory was that a horse had once knocked over his bike and buckled the wheel. The incident was compounded by the fact that the bike was not his! The absence of bodies meant that the grieving families had nowhere to go to pay their respects. This led to the advent of cenotaphs, of which there are 33,000 in Britain.

In my early years, when immunisation was much less comprehensive than it is now, childhood diseases were rampant. I well remember the dreadful cough that heralded measles. It was the kind of cough that made the parents bring their child in on the day it started. Then a rash appeared on the fourth day. But in 1977, a different type of cough appeared which I had never heard before – whooping cough. The campaign against the whooping cough vaccine, later to be discredited completely, led to a population that lost its herd immunity. Later studies showed that the long-term consequences of whooping cough were not as bad as it was feared, but at the time, it was grim. A child would start coughing; after two weeks, the glue-like sputum would cause the child with a brisk cough reflex to cough until it resulted in a desperate, inhalatory whooping cough. Vomiting was part of this infection, and it would go on for another four weeks before tailing off two weeks later – two months of hell! I found that Mucodyne (Carbocysteine, given to thin down the secretions in people with cystic fibrosis) would relieve the whoop and the vomiting in a day, but three days after stopping it, the cough would all come back. However, some relief was better than nothing.

The effect of whooping cough, because of its prolonged presence, was brought home to me in stark fashion. Our house was situated in front of a forest, and one day, we had decided to take the children out there for a walk. As I opened the back gate, a lady walked by. She stopped abruptly and stared at me intently, which is when I recognised that she was our old neighbour, Mrs Tucker. I had not seen her for probably thirty years. *"You're Charles, aren't you?"* she said suddenly. I replied that I was. *"You gave our Heather whooping cough when you were six months!"* she said and then she walked on. I never saw her again. The time her daughter had caught the whooping cough was vivid in her memory; a thirty-year gap had not lessened the resentment. One of my daughters had caught whooping cough at six months, and during the two months of the cough, she had vomited over every visitor and piece of furniture we had.

Infectious diseases were part of being a family doctor and seemed to strengthen our immunity and prevent illnesses. Decades of being coughed on, sneezed on, vomited on – not to mention the diarrhoea – must have done some good. I have to say that the patients were terribly thoughtful in that it had never occurred to them that they might give us something!

In December 1989, we had a real flu epidemic, and I remember it well, although sometimes, I wonder if anyone else does. I was doing, as my diaries record, about fifteen visits a day. Hardly anyone came to the surgery, so the workload was about the same. The new hospital at Bournemouth had just opened, and it bore the brunt just as the older hospital at Poole had done in East Dorset for the past many years. Two wards were closed at Poole, and a host of nurses were off duty due to illness. The tragic part I remember is that because of a patient overload, those with illnesses other than the flu were neglected, and everyone was treated as though they had the flu. Thus, we lost a man to acute pancreatitis and a lady with inappropriate antidiuretic hormone secretion, both of which were eminently treatable.

In 2009, we were warned of the advent of the swine flu, and this introduced a situation I found to be quite sinister. I believed that we were witnessing a precursor of the shutdown of our economy and the limitation of our freedom as we know it today. Instead of doctors ministering to their patients, the central government controlled everything. First, we were told that each practice had to draft an action plan. This stimulated reflection, but just as we put our reflection and local knowledge into words, a template appeared to do the job for us. It was presumably thought up by some manager who was responsible for drawing up meaningless templates. It commanded that we appoint a lead. It is one thing to appoint a leader for, say, diabetes or mental health, but quite another for an epidemic. What would happen if the lead was ill? There was no advice in the template. Surely the obvious thing to do would be for all the partners and leaders in the practice to meet at 8.30 am each day and plan the fight. If one was ill, no matter – the rest would continue. The question of what we would do if the lead was ill and the suggested solution drew no response. Central control was paramount. The possibility that the key workers might fall ill had not occurred to them. One such section of key workers that I worried would be affected was the tanker drivers. A few years ago, we had endured a tanker drivers' strike and, very quickly, the petrol stations had closed. What if the tanker drivers caught the flu? How would we visit the sick? But being a family doctor had its advantages. The manageress of my nearest petrol station and her family were my patients. While chatting with her, I found that to avoid contamination in the petrol, they close the pumps when they are still one-third full. In fact, they have plenty of petrol. Thus, I was able to continue home visits during the strike with no trouble. Was the health authority aware of this? How would doctors visit without petrol? But they were not interested; they had total control.

Our phones were to deliver a message to all incoming calls, warning them of the possibility of flu and informing them whether or not they should have Tamiflu. What was Tamiflu? I had never heard of it and nor had anyone else to start with. There was an anti-viral drug, Relenza but this was now ignored in favour of Tamiflu. Both were neuraminidase inhibitors.

Years later, its use was discredited, and its enormous cost was revealed. But for every patient who rang in during the summer of

2009, the only question to be considered was whether they should take Tamiflu. One such call came through to me one Wednesday afternoon. It was the husband of a woman whom I had attended her home delivery twenty-five years previously. He asked if she should have Tamiflu, and I asked about the symptoms. At this point, it would have been easier to say yea or nay and put the phone down. But I listened and the whole thing sounded strange and unlike the flu. I asked her to come down. On listening to her and examining her, it was clear she was ill, but I was not exactly sure why. She hadn't passed much urine, but if she was ill, she might not have been drinking much fluid. I took her blood and said I would call the next day. The results came back; she had acute renal failure. She was admitted immediately, dialysed and went on to do a kidney transplant.

The controlling nature of and over-reaction by the authorities led to the mildest but (at that time) most expensive epidemic in the history of the human race. COVID-19 may not be as mild, but it will be infinitely more expensive. Also, the control which was exhibited in 2009 has become intolerable in 2020. Social distancing is being observed at large but the police have been admonishing ordinary, solitary people who are exercising. While cycling in the New Forest, we saw a policeman; I had never seen a policeman in the forest before placing stickers on solitary cars. Had all crime been suspended? A few weeks previously, the police said they were so busy that they could only deal with serious crime! House sales have frozen, but the Land Registry Office telephone informed us that we cannot contact them due to increased workload because of the virus. They have no workload! It is all very strange to me when I hear of doctors isolating themselves because of some minor association with the disease. For forty-seven years, I was face to face with patients who coughed, sneezed, vomited and dribbled over me. And don't forget the sputum and diarrhoea! Was it nerve-wracking and uncomfortable? Yes, it was! But we never cut and ran.

In the 19th century, without knowing what a virus was and with precious little information on bacteria, diseases were controlled with sanitation and quarantine. We now have physical distancing and hand washing as preventive measures; so, did we need a lockdown? What we did need to do was quarantine the people who came into the country and trace their contacts. What we should not have done was send the elderly COVID-19 cases back to ill-equipped care homes. If we had been at war, this would have been called a war crime! We should not have admitted patients with infectious diseases at the general hospitals. They should never have got past A&E. We probably do not have infectious diseases' hospitals now, but we could have made isolation units. Typically, science hides behind the R number – the number of cases one infected person infects. It is a surrogate marker beloved by doctors and scientists. It makes them sound as though they understand it all. It makes a killer disease the property of the leadership rather than the other way round. It is easier to talk about the surrogate marker than the individuals who suffered and died. Who is in charge? Are they ever brought to justice? Yes, I do know the answer to that! Many years ago, I had two elderly ladies as patients who were admitted for minor procedures. But they acquired Norovirus in the hospital, and because they thrashed around with violent diarrhoea and vomiting, they sustained abrasions that were then infected with MRSA. Finally, they both died of MRSA septicaemia. They had entered the hospital thinking it would be a place of safety and found it to be a source of infection which then killed them. This was all because someone thought that hospital cleanliness contracts should be given to the lowest bidder! Hospital cleanliness should surely go to the organisation that will best be able to sanitise it. The monetary burden of reversing Norovirus and MRSA was colossal; the human cost, pitiful.

One extraordinary finding is that every medical mishap in this epidemic has been blamed on the government. Where was NHS England during this and the £28 billion they consumed which never comes out? Our NHS is appallingly centrist and controlling. As I write today on April 24, 2020, of the 100,000 beds in the NHS, 45,500 are unoccupied! And yet, a few months ago, the NHS was said to be overloaded with work. All the staff work "long hours." They are all heroes. The greatest myth of all is that they work harder than their predecessors did. That is a barefaced lie but is used as a lever to get more pay from the government. When I first started in 1970, I knew that no one in their right mind would work for the NHS, and yet, I did for forty-seven years. The NHS is a sacred cow, and I did not ever think that this sacred cow could trash our economy. Our PM, Boris Johnson, who I admire, chose "Save the NHS" as his slogan. But hang on, shouldn't the NHS be saving us?

STRANGE INFECTIONS

O NE DAY, A LADY HAD come in with a lump in her groin. It was an enlarged lymph gland that was only slightly tender. Painless, enlarged lymph glands are worrying, but tenderness suggests infection somewhere in the gland drains. There was no sign of infection, but as the days went by, it got bigger and bigger. Routine blood tests were conducted, but eventually, it threatened to burst, and I referred her to a hospital where a biopsy was done. The verdict was cat scratch fever. At that time, the causative organism, a bacterium named Bartonella, had not yet been identified or named. I had not asked her if she had a cat because it had never occurred to me. Doctors are not keen on home visits, and yet, if I had done one, I would have seen that she lived with twenty-four cats! That's a bit of a clue there. The New Forest Wildlife Centre informs that the disease is still about and had killed a veterinary nurse last year.

George was our goalie and a very good one. One day, his wife had rung me up to say that he had a temperature. Indeed, he did – 103°F on the old thermometers. He was sweating profusely but, otherwise, showed no other physical signs of illness, and so, I said I would review him in a few days. On the next visit, he was the same and not otherwise ill. We rarely admitted anyone to the hospital then, so I offered to review him once more. Also, one simply did not admit a case with an infectious disease at a general hospital, as was done during this COVID-19 epidemic. The next visit found him still pyrexial at 103°F; so, I took his blood for serology. The result came back stating that he had Q fever. Q fever is a rickettsial disorder like Typhus. Although a bacterium, rickettsia-like viruses can only survive in living tissues. It can be acquired from cattle, sheep and goats, but George had had nothing to do with any of those. He had worked in a rural village, but the closest thing he had come into contact with were some horses, which he had kept away from. It was a mystery but one that had given him a temperature of 103°F for ten days.

People could be extraordinarily forgetful about what they had done. Once, a man had come in with a huge viral-looking wart on the back of his hand. I asked him whether he had come in contact with any animals even though I was unaware of any connection, and he denied it. A few weeks later, I saw his sister and asked her whether her brother was alright and whether he had contact with animals. She revealed that the lambing was just over, and her brother often had to feed them by hand! Mystery solved! He had Orf!

On a different note, I had once been approached by a headmaster with a bowel problem; so, I mentioned the colonoscopy he had had the previous November. He denied any such procedure. We discussed it at length but he was in full denial. It is easy to forget all sorts of things, I would allow, but a six-foot tube up your backside! I think the procedure had been so unpleasant that his mind had wiped the slate clean.

FUNNY MOMENTS

M OST DOCTORS SHARE A LOVE–HATE relationship with home visits, but one thing on the good side is being able to look at the old photos. When you grow old, you may look older, but in your head, you are the same as you ever used to be. You know it, but the other person may not. When you look at old snaps on a patient's mantelpiece, you get a real idea of who you are dealing with. Often, there were photos of men in uniform or marriage photos. I found it fascinating to know about their military background. For example, Mr Lewis had been in the second Chindits. I doubt if this information would mean anything to doctors now, but I was familiar with the Burma campaign. I had another patient who had been with Orde Wingate's first Chindits. He was thin and wiry and looked just like those men in the old wartime films on their campaign. On the other hand, Mr Lewis did not look thin or wiry and had seen a fair bit of action. He was over ninety and had heart troubles due to which twenty stents had to be inserted. Despite everything, he was symptomless, and his wife, a stoical and pragmatic woman of ninety, confided in me that she thought he was a hypochondriac. I thought that a man who had lived so long and seen so much should be given the benefit of the doubt.

One day, the practice received a notification from Poole A&E that Mr Lewis had been taken in as an emergency case but had died on arrival. The next day, I rang up his wife to express my commiserations and ask how she was coping and whether she needed any help. She was as stoical and pragmatic as ever, and we had a nice chat, but she said there was nothing she needed me to do. A few weeks later, I felt I should check on her again. I called her and again, we had a pleasant chat about her and her late husband. She remained stoical and there seemed nothing for me to do.

A few weeks after that, I was in the treatment room, pottering about as usual, when Mr Lewis and his wife stepped out of one of the cubicles. For an instant, I froze. He was dead. The walking dead! He walked past me as he never said much, but his wife and I exchanged pleasantries. I had had two bereavement phone calls with her! Whatever must she have been thinking? Did she just think I was stupid and was too polite to say the truth? I was too embarrassed to follow it up. We then rang up Poole A&E, who checked and then said it had been a mistake – no explanation, no apology, just a mistake.

Travellers were always fun, and we always got along well with them, partly as they hadn't settled next door! One day, I saw that John was next on the list. I went out to call him and returned to my room. There was no response, so I called out again. *"I'm just waiting for the wife,"* he said with pride in a distinctly Irish accent. He was eighteen, and behind him was a very attractive young girl of about sixteen. He introduced me to her. On conducting the examination, I found he had a raging follicular tonsillitis, and I took a swab and prescribed penicillin. A week later, an older man came in, also accompanied by an attractive young girl. *"I want another prescription for my painkillers."* I asked him why he needed them, expecting him to describe some painful problem. *"My son got married last week."* *"Ah,"* said I, *"that wasn't John by any chance?"* He confirmed it was. The boy I had met the previous week was his son. There had been a wedding, which had gone on for two days, after which they had started fighting, which was when he had lost his prescription. It was all said as though it was the most natural thing in the world to begin fighting after two days and lose a prescription as a normal consequence. *"But why do you need the painkillers?"* I asked. *"My toe,"* he replied and revealed a gangrenous big toe. The young girl now intervened. *"Why does it smell like that,"* she demanded. It did smell pretty rank. I explained that was what dead and rotting toes smelt like. *"There you are,"* said the man turning on her, *"I told you they were meant to smell like that!"* He was triumphant, and she was suppressed. I enquired why the toe was gangrenous at all, and he explained that he had been a heavy smoker, his arteries had been blocked and he had required urgent surgery. At this point, he opened his shirt and revealed a vertical abdominal scar from his sternum down to his pubis with another horizontal scar right across his belly. Someone had performed heroic surgery, presumably for what is known as a saddle thrombosis, one which involves the aorta and both iliac arteries, thus cutting off the supply to both legs. His legs had been saved for the loss of just one big toe, which was now gangrenous and ready to fall off someday. I was mesmerised by the stoical way in which he had taken all this, and at the moment, all I could offer was, *"Well, at least you don't smoke now."* I mumbled this despite the distinct smell of tobacco. *"No, no,"* he replied, and then, as though he knew what I could smell, he added, *"but the wife does, twenty-five a day; I send her out to the shed!"*

WIMBORNE ROAD

"*O*LD *VIDLER NEEDS A HOME visit; he can't get his boots on!*" announced my secretary at the end of morning surgery one day. I did not know Old Vidler, and I was surprised any of the staff did because when his Lloyd George envelope was brought in, it was practically empty except for his date of birth, which revealed he was ninety-four! It seemed as though he had gone through ninety-four years of his life without any medical interventions.

All the medical notes are computerised now, but back then, they were stored (or not stored) in a beige envelope dating back to the advent of medical care, which was devised by Lloyd George. If maintained carefully, they were surprisingly efficient. On the outside, the envelope held an extraordinary amount of information. Apart from the written notes by the doctors, which were used as an aide memoir, there was a pink sheet for problems to be recorded and a blue sheet for drugs. The name of the drug and its starting and ending dates could be written where appropriate. Thus, at a glance, the drugs a patient was on was clear as was the drugs they had been on and, where appropriate, why they had been stopped. The problem card was also clear, and the doctor could write about not only illnesses and diseases but also major life events, such as births, bereavements, divorce, etc. This gave a real picture of the patient at a glance. Major conditions, such as diabetes and hypertension were represented by a sticker on the outside of the notes. Letters were folded and placed inside the envelope. This was quickly filled without careful culling. Thus, repeat appointment letters, letters without a date, letters in which the name of the patient was wrong or unclear, were all shredded. The current computers, thanks to their ability to do so and to the medical defence unions, scan and record everything. And I mean *everything*. The result is a virtually unreadable record of irrelevant information. Every piece of information, however irrelevant, is retained, and the result is a huge barrier of digital rubbish between the doctor and the patient. How many times have patients rightfully bleated "all they did was look at the screen"? As time went on and with an ageing population and co-morbidities, some practices went back to folders. A few years ago, I spent a year culling about 800 such folders and computerising their notes. All the letters and paperwork were filed in the newly available space. Thus, all the documents culled in the Lloyd George envelopes were filed to make a thick, unreadable tome. The tone for the computerised age was set: throw your brains and common sense out of the window but never throw away a medical document!

No such barrier existed in the case of Old Vidler; the only obstacle was that there wasn't much to proceed with in the notes. When I visited him, I saw a very old but still feisty gentleman with swollen ankles that prevented him from putting his boots on. He had been widowed nineteen years previously and had lived alone ever since. He held an acre of ground on which he grew anything he could; I could see broad beans, runner beans, fruit trees, cabbages and lettuce all in neat patches with barely any fallow ground left. After ninety-four years of toiling and good health, he had gone into heart failure, and his ankles had swollen with oedema, which prevented the boots from going on. After a long chat, during which all I really learnt about him was his resilient nature, I treated him with a water tablet and, possibly, digoxin for his heart, and over the next week, his condition improved, and he managed to get his boots on. The onset of heart failure in a ninety-four-year-old is pretty terminal, and he only lasted a year or two.

The point was that old Vidler was not alone. As time passed by, I discovered more of such characters down Wimborne Road, who had lived long lives and had unblemished medical histories, (and empty envelopes). It reached a stage where I honestly believed that if one wanted a long – and probably uneventful – life, one should live down on Wimborne Road. Of course, they have all gone now, but I wonder why they were so healthy in an age of rarely effective medical interventions. It was apparent to me in the 70s that when a man over seventy was ill, it was his last illness. Within a few decades, you could not even say that in the late 80s because, although they lived longer, it was not always in good health. These old, rural characters lived long and had good health. But I often think, are there Wimborne Roads all over the country? Probably.

I discovered such people from time to time, but I once made an interesting but slightly different discovery down Wimborne Road. One morning, ambulance control said they had been called to an elderly lady and asked if I could visit. She lived less than a mile from the centre of Clayford, alone in a bungalow on ten acres of land. Land and buildings in Clayford were at a premium, so how this large area had survived was intriguing. As I entered the property, I could smell the dankness and lifelessness of old neglected buildings. There were also very large cobwebs, which, to me, meant very large spiders! The lady in question was seated in a chair, and it was not clear what the problem was or why the ambulance had been called. There was no sign of an active kitchen, so how she managed to look so well-nourished was another conundrum, followed by why she was unknown to the practice. She began to tell an interesting story, and the photographs on the wall confirmed it. During WW2, some of Dorset was requisitioned by the war department for tank and artillery use before the D-Day landings. One such place was a village called Tyneham in Worbarrow Bay. In 1943, the whole village had been moved out, with only a month's notice, after each household had been sent a letter. The villagers, 225 of them, were heartbroken and pinned a notice on the church saying they would return one day. Alas, the War Department made the decision permanent in 1948, and the villagers never got their homes back. However, the village has now been fairly restored, and not only the church, but the school is also in good condition, and access is granted at prescribed times. In the school, there are two photographs of classes of children. One has the names of all the children but the other does not. On the far left of that one sat a little girl, who looked very much like the lady seated in front of me. I only ever knew her as Miss Bristowe. She had lived in Tyneham until 1943 when the village was cleared. She had an uncle, who sounded pretty well off and had property in Clayford. He moved her there, and there she had stayed. As her health declined, the lady across the road brought food in for her. Fish and chips seemed to be responsible for her good nourishment. So, was she the little girl in the picture? I believe she was, but there was no mention of anyone called Bristowe in the school or village. However, there are many photographs in Tyneham Farm next door which show that the family had a young girl companion named Bristowe. I hope I am not doing her a disservice by saying that she was probably not the brightest girl, but in that old village, she at least had a place. She lived many years in a home in Clayford, and I regret I never talked to her again about her intriguing origins. Thousands of people visit Tyneham each year and hear the sad story of the 225 villagers who were displaced, but they probably never think of what became of those people. Was my old lady one of them? Was she the young girl in the picture? If ever you visit Tynham, walk down to Worbarrow bay and you will realise why you would never want to live anywhere but Dorset!

LAKE WOBEGON?

Y OU MAY BE FAMILIAR WITH those wonderful radio recitals by
Garrison Keeler on the tales of Lake Wobegon. It was a place
in Minnesota where everyone was ordinary apart from the children,
who were all above average. People who showed themselves up were
looked down on, and the main virtue in life was to last. In fact, if
one died prematurely, which meant at less than seventy years, it was
almost as though one had let the side down. There were times when I
thought Clayford was like that. The people were happiest when nothing
happened and, like Lake Wobegon, when it did, they were either in
denial or diverted the event to something banal. My sister, who lived
in Clayford for most of her life, was very much like that. She insisted
that nothing happened down her road, oblivious to the young couple
opposite to her who both died of different cancers or the lady a little
further up with schizophrenia or the man trading drugs along the road.
Nothing ever happened in Clayford, and she would have been horrified
if anything did.

Once, a patient of mine went to visit his estranged wife and two
children, but she did not let him in further than the doorstep. When the
visit was over, he went to his car, parked on the road, filled it with petrol
and set it alight. There was a big explosion, and his wife and, probably
his children too, came out to see the huge fire that just about destroyed
the car as well as the man. It was awful. How do you get over that? But
a few weeks later, I overheard two ladies discussing it, and through their
voices, I could hear Garrison Keeler droning on in his soft Minnesotan
accent, *"the Council will never get that black mark off the pavement."* This
was the place I spent my career!

MINOR ILLNESS

T HERE IS MUCH MINOR ILLNESS in General Practice. One of the
roles of a GP is to identify minor illnesses and deal with them.
That is why it is fundamental that a GP is able to recognise what is
and is not within the realms of normality. Recognising what is normal
sounds terribly simple, but as any budding young doctor can tell you,
it is not. Likewise, nurses with limited, albeit good, medical training
face difficulties when presented with challenges outside their speciality.
Babies who always lie on one side temporarily develop misshapen
heads, but when faced with such a head and an anxious mother, one's
confidence drains. When a fourteen-year-old comes in with his Dad due
to unilateral gynaecomastia, the condition is not an issue, but the anxiety
is. When a girl of similar age comes with her mother due to unilateral
gynaecomastia and requests its removal, it's a medical disaster. The
number of people who discover their inions (the pointy bit at the back of
the skull) or their Xiphisternum (which sometimes protrudes at the base
of the breastbone in their middle age is surprising! All these are within
the realms of normality, and when the old family doctor said it was
normal, it usually was. But if the modern doctor, who is unfamiliar to
the patient, says so, there will be pressure for a referral – an unnecessary,
time consuming and expensive referral. Providing reassurance was one
of the roles taken up by the family doctor, but the modern patient is
reluctant to be reassured. This adds to the doctor's frustration, but that
is one of the prices to be paid while being a portfolio doctor.

Three very common benign conditions that spring to the mind are
sebaceous cysts (more accurately called inclusion dermoids), lipomas and
fibroids. Sebaceous cysts grow from the grease glands that grease the
hairs and are full of rank smelling white stuff. Lipomas are bodies of

fat in a sac that lies in subcutaneous fat. Fibroids are fibre and muscle ball-like bodies in the wombs of older ladies. They are all very common and benign (though fibroids can cause pain and bleeding). But over the years, I have seen a sebaceous cyst become a squamous cell carcinoma (very nasty), a lipoma become a reticulum cell sarcoma (nastier) and a fibroid also become a reticulum cell sarcoma. This encapsulates the conundrum of general practice; most things are benign or self-limiting, but every now and again, lightning strikes. If you work in a specialist department, the incidence of serious issues will be high and so will the index of suspicion. In general practice, the index of suspicion has to be low, otherwise, the referral rate would be sky high and the anxiety engendered by the doctor to the patient would also be high. But if you haven't had enough experience to confidently offer reassurance, how do you reassure someone? In this scenario, the comfort of reassurance, not to mention the placebo effect of the doctor, is lost.

One relatively minor complaint is the BCC – the basal cell carcinoma. It is the least malignant of the skin cancers and, fortunately, does not metastasise – seed to other sites. It also has another name – the rodent ulcer! As the name suggests, it can eat away the skin like a gnawing rat. Unfortunately, they appear in two varieties: the nodular, which can be removed easily and completely, and another variety with roots. Like the Japanese knotweed, removing the top is purely temporary as it comes back more extensively later, although, in the case of the BCC, this may take twenty to thirty years. Thus, I always reassure the patients with the first signs that "we have time on our side."

'Snobby' Rose had developed such a BCC when a young man. Snobby, I was told, was a local Dorset word for a cobbler, but I don't have confirmation of this information. The internet says it is a naval term and stands for number one boot specialist, which shows the connection to cobbling. Snobby had had a BCC on his face for years, and whether the treatment had been delayed or unsuccessful, I never knew. As time went on, it eroded one ear, his face and then the orbit; so one of his eyes had to go. This resulted in a huge cavity (I advise the reader to read my words but not to imagine what it looked like). To make Snobby presentable in public, a prosthetic half-face had been fashioned. It was not terribly good but better than the alternative. This needed cleaning out frequently by the district nurse, who observed one day that, when he blew his nose, pus shot out of one ear! To clean everything out, she had to remove the prosthesis, of course, and clean it separately. Snobby had got used to it and did not give it a second thought. One day in the middle of the procedure, which took place at his home, the postman arrived with a parcel and knocked on the door. Snobby got up and answered it! The DN was phlegmatic: "Another patient, a vomiting collapsing postman – all in a day's work."

ON-CALL

W HEN I HAD STARTED, WE were on-call an awful lot during nights and weekends. We had a rota, of course, but time flew quickly and one's turn came round much too soon. When I had started, a weekend on duty began on Friday morning and went on to the following Monday evening. When my daughter started as a doctor and had her first weekend on duty with two other doctors for 500 patients in a hospital in London, I asked if she had reached the stage of never wanting to see another patient again. She said no, but I reassured her that she would one day. It had happened only five times in forty-eight years, but I remember those moments well. It occurred once on a Monday night after a weekend. I should add that the calls came through to our landline at home day and night, so there was no escape. And when I was out, my wife was the doctor! Therefore, early on, I had decided to do an experiment. For one weekend, I had decided to be as nice and helpful as possible, to make follow-up phone calls where appropriate and, in general, be all things to all people. The next weekend that I was on, I did the exact opposite. I did as little as possible, whilst still being good, and operated in a professional but surly way. In the end, I reflected as objectively as possible, whilst acknowledging that true objectivity was impossible. The helpful doctor was exhausted, but the grumpy doctor was still energetic and ready for more. It taught me a good lesson: You always have to be good, but do you always have to be nice? Now, doctors have to be nice all the time, even to the time-wasters, the downright rude and the odious. They have to be nice to those who are outright hostile too. No wonder they suffer from burn out and exhaustion and have to go on resilience courses. It may be of great merit to be all things to all people, but believe me, you won't last!

We always had a rota, but as time went on, it became more benign. After six years, I was the senior partner and was able to choose Monday as my weeknight on duty. I well remember those Monday nights. One of the perverse issues with being on-call was the love–hate relationship with it. We did not look forward to it, especially going to bed knowing that any phone call would almost certainly pitch you out of bed for an hour and a half at the minimum. It was not very good for our sleep cycle. But the next day, the doings of those calls would be all you wanted to talk about. And here I am, thirty to forty years later, reciting them again!

Lilah and her husband were as close to Hyacinth Bucket as one could get. She was large, loquacious and snobbish, and he was quiet, loyal and attentive. He had been a harbour master at Ostend during WW2, but that must have been easy compared to looking after Lilah. She was, it has to be said, a wonderful lady but always full on. In fact, many, if not most, of my patients liked talking to me and listening came a poor second. One evening at about 6 pm, her hubby had rung me to say that Lilah had not been eating much and to enquire whether he should give her insulin. She had had type 2 diabetes for years and was now maintained on insulin. As it was the end of a long day, I may not have taken it all in, so I had told him to go ahead, knowing that I would be on call that evening, and if anything went wrong, I would have to take care of it. At 7 pm, the phone rang at home. *"I think Lilah may be dead."* One thing I learned early on from being on-call was that when the caller says that the patient "cannot breathe at all", they were probably breathing well, but when they say the patient "is only breathing very little", they have probably been dead for hours. However, I knew that Lilah may have had gone hypoglycaemic due to the insulin, which was why she looked like she was lifeless. I was around in minutes and administered intravenous Dextrose 50%, as we did in those days. It had a dramatic effect and did not disappoint us. From being completely moribund, the corpse sat up and gushed, *"Oh, Dr Rees, I'm so glad you're here. Don't send me to the hospital; I don't want to go to the hospital. I hate that new Bournemouth hospital; the bannisters are all painted a dreadful colour of red, and I hate that colour, and the last time I was in, the nurses spent all their time talking at their station and not bothering about me, and it was all because they had examinations the next day, and how they were going to get on...."* Try being unconscious one second and then, in a heartbeat, saying all that in one breath. She could talk for England. On several occasions she called at the end of morning Surgery. I would start listening and without even making listening noises, sign all my prescriptions and take messages and when finished pick up the phone again to hear her still talking! I had seen a whole generation of people like her. I thought they were funny at the time, but when they passed on, I experienced a real sense of bereavement.

Another Monday night regular was Franksy. He was a young man, under thirty, who had issues with drugs – not a huge problem at that time – and alcohol. He also had mental health issues, and they aggravated each other. People who drink a lot become resistant to alcohol. Unfortunately, at the same time, it makes them resistant to anti-depressants. Every now and again, his mental health issues, drug abuse and alcohol consumption would come to a head. Then, a doctor would be called, and although all my partners were involved, Monday nights seemed to be his favourite time to go off. He lived with his mother, an attractive but somewhat aloof and uncooperative woman. She behaved more like an annoyed landlady than a mother and cohabited with a man who, I believe, owned the rather nice-looking bungalow they lived in. Having Franksy lumber around the place like a bull in a china shop must have tried his equilibrium. As an aside, no-one grew tomatoes like him. On the occasions where a doctor was called, Franksy would be out of his mind and, apparently, crashing around the house. But an examination of the patient includes their environment, and I noticed that the ornaments were never smashed, and a fine model of a large boat, which would have taken months to build, was never in danger. There was a good deal of manipulation in his behaviour, and deep down, he knew what he was doing. On this particular occasion, the situation was utterly out of hand, and I arranged his admission to a mental hospital. It was never easy to do this, but it was especially difficult when they knew it was Franksy. On this particular night, he had, on top of everything else, swigged a litre of red wine and vomited most of it down his front. Eventually, when an ambulance arrived, there stood Franksy, suddenly quite calm, and his front covered in vomit, dribble and wine. He turned to me suddenly and said *"Thank you so much, Doctor, for being so helpful"*. And then, he gave me a big hug, leaving the wine, slaver and vomit down my front. Thank you, Franksy!

One of the joys of being called up while on duty was the complete uncertainty of what would greet you. One evening, I had received a call from a shaky sounding old lady. *"Can you come and see Dennis; he's having one of his turns."* Being new to the practice, I knew nothing of Dennis or his turns and made inquiries on whether he was epileptic, had any heart troubles, and the like. All the questions produced vague answers, so off I went. We always tried some rearguard action in the hope we might avoid a home visit but never with much hope. When I arrived, I was greeted by the old lady and a huge man and lady who, it turned out, were the siblings of the patient in question. *"What is the problem?"* I inquired. They clearly expected me to know all about Dennis and were amazed that I didn't. *"So, you don't remember the last time Dennis had a turn?"* I knew nothing. *"The last time when the old doctor came out and we had to call the police (my attention was seized at the mention of the police) and he put three of them in the hospital."* They had my complete attention at this point. He had had a turn and put three policemen in the hospital! I quietly asked what was expected of me. *"Maybe you can talk to him,"* they replied. But about what!

With the kind of bravado and foolishness that had caused me a lot of trouble over the years, I asked to be shown to him. They walked me to a bedroom. They were clearly a big-boned family, but I will never forget the tingling I felt as I walked through the door to see the end of a bed with two feet sticking out at least a foot beyond the end! As I bid farewell to my life, a quiet voice said, *"Hello, Doctor,"* in an East Dorset accent. *"Hello, Dennis,"* I replied with some relief. We talked. It was not clear what was wrong but talking was better than being put in hospital. Dennis had had a pituitary tumour years ago, and although surgery had removed the tumour, it had left him blind. He lived with his mother and fine-tuned radios that the local people brought to him. Still, with the thoughts of the hospitalised police in my mind, I suggested giving him something to calm him down. He concurred. He was definitely big, so I drew up Diazepam 20mg and injected it into his elbow vein very slowly. *"There,"* I said, *"you will be fine now. You will fall asleep and, tomorrow, all will be well."* Relieved and triumphant, I went out and reported the same to the mother and siblings. As I glowed reflecting on a job well done, a gentle voice came from the bedroom. *"Doctor."* What! He was awake? *"Er, yes Dennis, what is it?"* *"Can I go to the toilet?"* I mumbled in the affirmative and, to my amazement and horror, Dennis got up, walked to the toilet and walked back again. The intravenous Diazepam had apparently had no effect on him whatsoever! He *did* sleep eventually, and he was fine the next day. In the years that followed, I had met and visited him many times, and we had had a good relationship. Strangely and mercifully, he had never had another 'turn' again.

One Monday morning in June at about 5 am, a man had called asking for a visit for his daughter. He was unclear about the problem. There may have been pain; there may have been bleeding – he was uncertain. Eventually, I told him that I did not want to get out of bed for a girl with period problems. He replied that he had been instructed by his wife to get the doctor and that was that. Indeed, it was. Losing all hope of completing a night's sleep and knowing that, whatever it was, I had another day's work to follow, I got dressed and drove off. It was a glorious, sunny June morning. When I arrived, the mother showed me upstairs with a similar lack of explanation. I had no idea what to expect, but as I walked through the bedroom door, I froze. This thirteen-year-old girl was not only pregnant, she was about to deliver the baby! *"Phone for an ambulance!"* I cried, but at that time, only 40% of homes had a phone, and this was not one of them. I don't think I have ever moved faster as I shot out to a phone box which was, fortunately, twenty yards away and begged for help. We used to carry all sorts of equipment, but a delivery pack was not one of them. The ambulance arrived and took the young girl away. The mother, for some reason, did not go with her and so, we stood and talked. *"I don't know what I am going to say to her father. We've been apart for the last four years, and he only came back last Friday."* I pondered for an answer and said, *"Tell him it was his fault!"*

A few houses away was another young girl who was pregnant. I used to visit them a lot because the mother had asthma. I was taken by the rough holes in the lower parts of all their doors. It was where their father kicked them, which, evidently, he did regularly. The mother and daughter were scared of him and even more so when the daughter became pregnant at fourteen. It is amazing how young girls, with their abdominal muscle tone, can hide the pregnancy. This girl added to the camouflage by wearing a baggy coat. She wore it throughout the pregnancy, summer as well as winter. Her father never noticed.

One call that senior partner, Jock, attended to is worth relating. I mention it because he greeted me on a Wednesday morning with the opening gambit *"Charles, you should have been on call last night."* Even now, I don't understand why he said that. When Jock had been on call the previous night, he had received a call from Golf Links Road – *"Can you come around, Doctor? My husband has cut himself in the bathroom."* No further information was given, and Jock was not a person to waste time on pleasantries. One of my friends went to see him. He said he had walked through the door and said he had a cough; Jock had him take his shirt off before he could even sit down. Good GPs survive by making an art form of taking short cuts. In this case, Jock shot around, and the lady pointed him to the bathroom. Her husband greeted him, and he held out a polythene bag containing his bloody testicles. He had castrated himself! Blood was pouring down both legs from his perineum. I believe he was schizophrenic, but what that explains, I am not sure. I saw him years later. The surgeon had done a very good job.

But not all my tales give me a feel-good factor. During general practice training, we are taught to ask ourselves if we could have done things differently. In this following case, I could have.

Trickett lived in a corner house on a council estate. He was a settled traveller whose family had seen better days. He carried a picture of his father, a big man in a waistcoat and a bowler hat, looking very pleased with himself, who evidently bought and sold horses. Trickett was a poor man but had a lovely personality. Unfortunately, he had married a schizophrenic wife and had a drug addict son. His son was frankly a toe-rag, and he had shacked up with a really weird woman. Nevertheless, Trickett embraced and cared for them all without judgement. That winter, two of my colleagues had been called out to see his wife in the evening, as always – they never called in the daytime – but they made no urgent request for follow up.

As I parked the car and approached the house, I could see it was pitch black. It turned out they had not paid their electricity bills. I knocked on the door and was welcomed into the living room. The room was full of rubbish, so it was not possible to move around. The sight that caught my attention was a huge, fiercely burning fire in the fireplace and, almost on top of it, a woman sitting in an armchair, She was so close it threatened to add her to the rest of the contents in the fireplace. Also, the rubbish in the room was mainly newspapers, boxes and generally flammable material. There was no other light source other than the fire, so seeing anything as one's pupils kept dilating and constricting was very difficult. I thought the woman may have looked pale and noted a rapid pulse, but there were no other signs of illness, and she was unhelpful. An added distraction was that my doctor's case was made of black plastic. It was normally very robust, but I had put a previous one too close to an electric fire once, and it had begun to melt. I did not want it to happen again, and I could feel the heat was only just bearable. I told Trickett that I would check her blood the next day, and he was content with this. I suspected she was anaemic but not critically so. The district nurse went to take her blood the next day and found the lady dead. In the post-mortem report, her haemoglobin level was 2 g per decilitre; the normal range was 12 to 15.5. I was mortified. She had what is known as cold agglutinins, which caused her to bleed, usually while passing urine, over a long period when cold. Trickett knew that she hated the cold, and hence, built a huge fire, which inadvertently acted as a deterrent to a proper examination. No-one suggested that I should have admitted her and, sadly, she was unmourned by her family.

HOME DELIVERIES

—

H AVING COMPLETED SIX MONTHS OF intensive obstetrics at Leeds Maternity Hospital, it seemed reasonable to continue home maternity in general practice. Clayford was expanding at that time, and babies were arriving thick and fast. I had a large antenatal clinic each week, and there were frequent deliveries. Many of them were at the Firs, a Maternity Hospital in Bournemouth; it was a lovely place, and the mums loved it. They were waited on hand and foot and would often stay for ten days. This was a luxury, and I sometimes wondered if ladies would become pregnant just for this ten-day holiday, as they used to refer to it. Now, mums are in and out in hours. Although the procedure at Firs would not be considered as a good medical practice now, the modern brevity in stay time is driven by finance and not good medical practice; so is much of our health service.

If a lady decided to deliver at home, I would always want to be there regardless of whether I was on call or not. That was part of being a family doctor more than just a GP. It was a privilege. Eventually, in 1998, I gave it up, but not because it was unsafe. A big problem with home delivery was that it was attracting the wrong kinds of mothers-to-be. Home delivery is ideal for a second, third or fourth pregnancy with an unblemished record. As far as I am aware, it is safe and does not attract dangerous hospital infections. Unfortunately, the ladies who demanded home delivery were often preparing for their first babies because they had been seduced by organisations that supported natural childbirth. They were primips – 'the untried vessels'. Due to the risks, the other doctors who usually did home deliveries refused to do them and I was increasingly asked to. Instead of one out-of-hours delivery every few months, it threatened to be as frequent as once a week on top of the usual on call.

Clearly, the situation has changed now. The mothers are heavier and the babies, bigger. The likelihood of problems is greater. The use of the caesarean section increased five-fold during the 90s despite its four-fold increase in maternal mortality and the likelihood of kidney damage due to blood loss. The art of delivery, which was so brilliantly taught by my mentor at Leeds, John Philips, has been lost. He was Welsh and lived for deliveries. There were many difficult births at LMH as they were the only ones they took. John would stalk the wards late at night looking for those poor women with long labours. He would sit with them and talk in his soft Welsh voice until, despite the pain and exhaustion, they were calm again. Then, he would gently apply forceps or a ventouse and manage the delivery. Thus, calm would prevail where there was panic and hopelessness. He did this most nights. He would appear like a ghost when things were at their worst. When all was done, he nearly always turned to the new mum and mischievously said, *"You will not realise the full significance of this for another eighteen years."* How true.

Some of John's calming effects must have rubbed off on me. One Saturday afternoon, I was at a grand fiftieth birthday garden party at the same place as the North American Bison (see earlier!). Suddenly a lady came up to me and said, *"Hello, Doctor! It's me, July; do you remember me?"* I did not at first. After twenty five years we had both aged! Then, it slowly dawned with some apprehension. It was twenty-five years ago. She was one of my home deliveries. I had been playing tennis one Saturday afternoon, but when I got home, the phone rang to say that all was well, July had delivered, but the placenta, the afterbirth, could not be removed. I shot round in seven minutes. Our super midwife and July were talking, and the baby was happy, but as she had said, all was well, but the wretched placenta was stuck! I gave it a pull but no luck. I examined to see how much was adhered to her and what the situation was. The patient, July, and the midwife chatted away non-stop and my examination seemed to give her no distress, so I carried on and began separating the placenta from the uterus slowly but surely. It seemed painfully slow at the time, but once I had started, I could see no reason to stop. It finally came away completely and that was that.

In retrospect, the thought of manual removal of the placenta outside a hospital with no blood available makes me cringe, but it seemed fine at the time. July was saved a trip to the hospital. The home delivery had been otherwise uneventful, and now, twenty-five years later, there she was and all was well.

There is one amusing sequel to this story. July and her mother, to earn a little money, had decided to set up a home help service, which they named Amy's home services after the above-mentioned baby. It, unfortunately, attracted the wrong sort of customer who was not looking for sweeping and polishing. One man, clearly not a gentleman, was delighted to be told that he could have both the mother and daughter for only £6 an hour!

One day, a new midwife, Philomena, had arrived. She was rotund, small, feisty and Irish. Above all, she hated home deliveries. Therefore, it was such a pity that she was forced to attend the most eventful home delivery of all time! It was on a Monday morning during one of our usual meetings that she appeared and began her tale of woe. She had been on call for the weekend and was called out to a delivery in the country. She was unfamiliar with the lady and circumstances and so, was walking into the unknown. It was a farm-like place, and the door was answered by the husband. He asked her to come upstairs, but instead of being shown into the bedroom, she was shown into the bathroom! The lady was to have a water birth, the husband explained. As much as Philomena did not like home births, she hated water births. Moreover, the bathroom was overcrowded: the patient was in the bath, moaning away, the husband was there, and so were two children from a previous marriage. For good measure, a neighbour, who was good at photography, was there to record the event. To add to the atmosphere, a cow was mooing outside in co-ordination with the mother-to-be. It was in this situation that Philomena completed the delivery of a boy. She vividly described the baby floating to the top of the bathwater mixed with blood and meconium, producing a macabre soup.

The baby was retrieved, placed in a blanket and passed to the husband after it had cried. At last, Phil could reach into the bathtub and pull the plug out. But a hand reached down beside her and put the plug back in – not yet! A bewildered Phil was taken downstairs to where a large saucepan-cum-cauldron was bubbling away full of foliage, branches, flowers and other stuff one would normally put in a compost heap. It was explained that since the baby and fluids – the fruits of nature – had left the mother, it had to be put back in! The cauldron was then taken to the bathroom and the contents poured in with the bloody, mucky bathwater. *"It was disgusting,"* said our new midwife. We agreed but believed she had stretched credulity. It was at this moment that she reached into her pocket and pulled out some photographs. *"They gave me these this morning when I went round."* Yes, credulity had been stretched, but truth beats fiction every time. She reassured us that the mother, baby and cow were doing fine.

MEDIEVAL MEDICINE

WHEN I LOOK BACK TO the medicine of the 1970s, I tremble at the paucity of effective medical interventions that were available to us. The great scourge of the time, for me, was rheumatoid and other forms of arthritis. It was crippling, unrelenting and, above all, painful. The suffering of our arthritic patients was awful and constant. The only treatments were aspirin and steroids. Steroids were usually given in doses that were far too high and produced as many problems as they alleviated. Some managed on very small doses of steroids and, years later, found that they had suffered very little long-term damage. But this information was not known at the time. I once had a woman on 16 x 300 mg aspirin a day. How her stomach endured it, I do not know, but she lived and functioned. Also, it was not known then that rheumatoid makes one predisposed heart disease with the inflammatory process probably affecting the coronary arteries and others.

One of my patients used to build swimming pools. One day, he announced that he had a new-fangled device called a jacuzzi. He said it 'offers a sense of well-being and cures all ailments,' and he marketed it as one would market snake oil off the back of a wagon in the old wild west. I discussed it with a patient, she was fifty-two and crippled with rheumatoid, and we decided to give it a go. I called for her, and it was a challenge to get her into my car and then out to where the jacuzzi stood in a large garage. Climbing up the steps and into the thing was another mission, but we did it and sat there for an hour, bubbling away. When it was time to get out, she was able to stand. She walked to the car, and on the way back, I asked her what she was going to do next. *I am going to comb my hair,* she said as she raised her right arm above her head. *I haven't been able to do that in years!*

The attitude to illness was also sometimes medieval. The idea that people were ill because of something they had done wrong was common, and it still exists. People with duodenal ulcers were admonished mercilessly for their lifestyle until it was found that the bacteria in their stomach, which was known about and discarded for eighty years, was, in fact, the cause of all their ills. It could be abolished with a cocktail of drugs and antibiotics in a couple of weeks. All that brilliant and developing surgery was unnecessary.

The idea that people are ill because of their own shortcomings still lurks in the minds of those whose default attitude is to scold. Shortly after I had retired, the wife of a friend had attended the surgery because she felt she was short of breath. She saw one of the practice nurses who immediately divined that it was because she smoked and was overweight. In fact, if she had known the family as I did, she would have known that this woman's lifestyle was exactly the same as that of her wonderful mother, Fluffy, who lived until she was ninety-three. She also had three dogs, which she exercised every day. She was then referred to a GP, who came to the same conclusion and referred her to a cardiologist. She then had a coronary angiogram, which turned out to be normal. It was only at this stage that a doctor listened to her and examined her. Again, if they had known her as a family doctor did, they would have known that she had no children and had never been on the combined contraceptive pill. A childless, middle-aged woman putting on weight, under those circumstances, should have rung alarm bells. The abdominal swelling was noticed, an abdominal ultrasound was performed, and eventually, the diagnosis of cancer of the ovary was made but too late.

Clinical governance compounds this medieval view that illness is the patient's fault. If you don't conform to the surrogate markers it is your fault. By designing a series of guidelines, it suggests that if one does not keep to those guidelines, then they are responsible for the consequences. The alcohol guidelines are particularly severe and, according to Professor Humphries of Stamford University in his paper on alcohol guidelines, uniquely so in the UK in the whole world! These have now been swallowed – no pun intended – by a generation of doctors who have never lived! Young doctors ask you about your drinking habits as though they are talking about crack cocaine!

DARK AND TENDER SECRETS

I DON'T THINK THE INDIGENOUS POPULATION of Clayford had any secrets. Information was transmitted by bush telegraph at high speed, aided by the fact that they all seemed to be related to one another. The secrets that existed among them were probably little secrets like who their real father was. I am still being made aware of family connections.

For the affluent and arrogant, their secrets were of a different level. Their relationship with us was different because, as we were not specialists, we were at the level of tradesmen. That was no problem to us, but their dark and tender secrets residing in the hands of tradesmen certainly was to them. Nearly all of them were golfers and, other than Jock, my old senior partner, none of my current partners were golfers. But life is a great equaliser. None of us is immune to events.

I found the ex-military and RAF patients in particular to be the most arrogant. One, in particular, continually admonished me, and even when I had saved his wife's life by preventing her from going on a six-week cruise instead of having her bowel removed, he insisted that I had *told her in the wrong way.* I think that, no matter what he knew about aeroplanes, he knew nothing of the human condition. His wife was a lovely lady, and as they could not have children, they adopted a girl. She grew into a stunningly attractive young woman. But although physically attractive, she was difficult to deal with and not to be crossed. I kept away from her, which, fortunately, was not difficult because she spent most of her time in Australia. Her adoptive parents were concerned when she had an affair with a man old enough to be her father and more concerned when they had their own child. The father was an Australian surgeon, and the relationship was tempestuous. They reported her tempers and violence, which her lover seemed to aggravate.

Her personality edged on psychopathic. Eventually, and painfully, they came in one day and revealed the awful truth. Their daughter's partner and lover – and the father of her child – was not only old enough to be her father, but he was her father!

The liaison was not accidental, which would have been unfortunate but innocent. The whole thing had been engineered by the doctor, who had deliberately seduced his own daughter. The dark and tender secret my patient had to live with at the golf club was that their daughter was a psychopath in an incestuous relationship. After that incident, the air vice-marshal was less contemptuous though still arrogant.

Another golfer, who was not only Scottish but living down a road named after a famous golf course, was of a similar mould as the AVM. His wife, on the other hand, was a lovely, mild and pleasant lady; these qualities had no doubt helped her relationship with her golfer husband. They had two children of their own, both grown up. One day, he brought her in for help. She was in a state of anxiety and depression. I listened. A week previously, a man in his forties arrived at their house. He told them that he believed he was her son. Thus, the story came out. Before she had met her husband, she had been in a relationship with someone – probably an American like hundreds of thousands of girls did – become pregnant, and delivered a baby that had then been given up for adoption. Clearly, the trauma to all – her, her husband, her children and her newly found child and his family – was immense. But as the months passed by, they all began to live with it, and the Scottish golfer settled back into his golfing life. He came to terms with it, and I applaud him for it.

A year later, they were back again. Unbelievably, another young man had turned up claiming to be her child. He was also adopted as the first one was. Of course, this was not funny in the least, but I could not help being reminded of the line in 'The Importance of Being Ernest' – "to lose one parent is unfortunate but to lose two sounds like carelessness." Lightening does not often strike twice. This time, the counselling was on another level. The stainless bride he had fallen in love with all those years ago had omitted to tell him that she had already had two children by two different men, their whereabouts unknown. There is only so much one can stomach. The Scottish golfer now had severe indigestion, but difficult or not, it was a dark and tender secret he had to take around the course.

One of the strangest secrets involved Jock, my senior partner. One day, I was called to visit a gorilla of a man. He lived in a very smart bungalow in an adjoining village with his slim and attractive wife who drove a pale blue Mercedes convertible. When I arrived, he was stripped to the waist and addressed me as "mush". It is not an uncommon form of address around here and comes from the Romany, meaning man. However, it was a bit unusual for me as a doctor to be a "mush." I spoke, as I often did, to Ian Limbery about this rough but pleasant character. Ian told me that many years previously, his wife had given birth to a daughter with spina bifida and, presumably, meningo-myelocoele and thus, paraplegia. She was apparently fairly damaged, and Jock told them she would not live and advised them to leave her in a home. Thereafter, they had nothing to do with her. However, his brother and wife, who were lovely, gentle people, brought her up. She lived, thrived, and one day, I saw her in a wheelchair. She was a highly capable and attractive young lady. The real parents remained in complete denial of her, and she expressed no desire to have anything to do with them. And as for Jock, according to Ian Limbery, he never knew that she had survived and grown into the wonderful person she was. Jock made a huge mistake but never knew.

PTSD

I N 1984, SOMETHING HAPPENED THAT had never happened before. It was the fortieth anniversary of D Day. Now, there is some sort of event of remembrance every year, especially as the veterans are dying out, and we all see the pictures on TV. In 1984, the thing that was different was that they were on TV for the first time. Every news channel said something about it, and the events of that momentous invasion were in every sitting room. This was new.

Following this, several older men came to see me, clearly depressed. One of my trainee doctors had suggested that it might be post-traumatic stress disorder. I confess I had never heard of it, but as I listened to the tales these men narrated, I believe she was spot on. One was a lovely man called Philip who had been a chemical engineer. He had been in the army and had been told that the Germans were moving large quantities of chemicals into numerous sites. He was to go in with the frontline forces and find out what they were doing. Presumably, it was some secret chemical weapon. Thus, on April 15, 1945, he and the accompanying troops walked straight into Bergen Belsen. No warning. No preparation. No inkling. He had suppressed this memory for forty years. But the pictures on the news had plunged him into an awful state of depression and nightmares as his memories had been released.

Another man had been thirty-nine on D Day and so was seventy-nine when he came in. He had been a British quartermaster attached to American units. They annoyed him because they always wanted a gross of everything, never just a few. They did not understand the shortages in wartime Britain. He was dropped in the water at Omaha Beach on D plus 3. Bodies floated all around him. He swam ashore and endured continuous action for ten days with gunfire, explosions and fire while surviving on little food and drink and being sleep deprived, after which he was relieved. That was his war. Ten days of hell. He too had suppressed it for forty years.

It is often said that veterans don't talk about their experiences, but many of them said that when they had tried, they got no response. I think it was because the listeners had no idea how to respond. As a result, the vets thought that they weren't interested and buried it. But only for so long. One man, who, it turned out, was beginning to dement and thus had less control over his mind, was haunted by an incident when he was in Burma. His unit was making progress but behind him was an injured Japanese soldier in a cave. The captain ordered him to go back and finish the soldier off, which he did. But all these years later, he was haunted by the thought that he had committed murder.

Almost at the end of the war, a member of his squad had trodden on a mine and he was the only one of five to survive, albeit injured. He was captured by the Japanese and thrown in a hospital bed with five others, all dead. On the way, they had passed two men who were crucified upside-down. He was soon rescued, but fate had another unfortunate experience that came back to haunt him. He was in the second Chindits and, eventually, evacuated by submarine. The submarine was attacked by one of our own, a destroyer from the Indian navy. For eighteen hours, they lay on the seabed as the engines went back and forth overhead with the occasional depth charge. A year later, when he went to a hotel in Torquay with a small room at the end of a long corridor and without, according to him, a window, the memories flooded back, and he went mad with acute anxiety.

And so, the stories poured in. These were the stories of peaceful men, taken from peaceful occupations, who had to endure a living nightmare. Their colleagues were the same, and they had put it behind them and got on with life until it was there, unasked for, in their living rooms on the fortieth anniversary of D Day. Great fun and pride for us, but for them, it a wakeup call for their nightmares. I remember six men who had been so affected, and they were all dead from cancer within a few years.

Strangely enough, after forty-eight years, when I finally retired from all the clinical work, I became quite depressed, and I wondered if it was a sort of PTSD. Forty-eight years of fighting in the National Health Service! No, I don't think so. There is a sort of – I am finding it very difficult to find the right words – comfort in caring for others. However, you may be feeling, when you get to work and sit down in front of the first patient for the day, you will quickly find someone worse off than yourself. Very quickly, you forget yourself and get on with the day. I wonder if that was the case and, maybe, I had suppressed so much over the years that was now emerging. These were not memories of the horrors of war, but these memories had plenty of disease, death, death sentences and the smells of the living, the dying and the dead which I have only hinted at here. Getting back on the job is said to be the treatment of PTSD, but that is not always possible. Another solution is to write it all down. So, I am!

MOST DIFFICULT TIME

O NE MIGHT THINK THE MOST difficult time a doctor would have to face would be caused by overload, the seriousness of a problem or the complexity of a challenge, but the most difficult time I went through was concerned with just one family. Charlie was an old soldier in his seventies. He had been in the Eighth Army and was exactly how one would imagine a soldier to be. He was small to average, fit, wiry and, when he first came in, fun. Unfortunately, that was the problem because his fun was due to hypomania. Manic depressive psychosis causes a person to alternate over weeks, months or even years between being high or low and depressed moods. The modern term is bipolar, but it has been adopted by people who are just fed up every now and again and who never go through the high phase. When Charlie was presented in a high mood, it was the first time I had seen him; so, I was unaware of his history. He had been sent in by his wife and this was part of the problem. Mrs Charlie did not like Charlie having fun! It became clear as time passed by that she much preferred him in his depressed state when she could control him. But now, he was fun. He had the usual forced speech and flight of ideas, but he was not all that bad. He would go to the bars around town, chat up ladies and spend money on them. He did not spend much, but it was not his usual habit. Mrs Charlie did not like Charlie spending anything and began pressuring me to have Charlie sectioned under the Mental Health Act. Frankly, he was a long way from that, but then, the son weighed in. The son was described by the private psychiatrist, who saw him regularly, to be Schizoid, whatever that was. I received long, hand-written letters after each consultation. Nothing ever changed, and I hadn't seen him until much later. He was definitely his mother's son. It was quite clear that the wife and son regarded Charlie's money as their money, and they were not going to allow any of it to slip away. They appeared regularly to tell me how I should manage Charlie. They threatened and cajoled in the surgery by phone and by letter. However, Charlie was my patient, and his well-being was my responsibility. I spoke to his accountant with his permission, who confirmed that Charlie was spending more than usual, but it was not outrageous, and he was a wealthy man anyway and could afford it. I encouraged Charlie to see a psychiatrist and accept treatment, but he was reluctant. People with hypomania are usually happy with their lot. They know that the dip into depression is likely and associate treatment with the onset of this miserable depression. Furthermore, Charlie found he could stand up to his wife and son when he was high. *"I fought a dictator for six years, and I am not being defeated by one now!"* was his mantra. So, I was the meat in the sandwich: squashed between my patient and his controllers. It was a surprisingly unpleasant experience, but Charlie eventually succumbed. He accepted treatment, calmed down and lost the will to fight. The last time I saw him, he was subdued and well in the control of his wife and son, who found a different doctor for him.

ASYLUM DUFF

C HARLIE WAS NEVER SO HIGH that he would cause damage to himself or others. When patients become really high, they are termed manic and can be a huge problem. When I worked as a student at High Royds Hospital, Menston, in the admission ward, a man was once brought in for stealing a bus and driving it around Leeds. When he came in, he was as high as a kite and would not listen to, let alone accept any treatment or management. How does one deal with such a problem? This is where experience counts. The charge nurse had dealt with such a situation before. I watched his technique in awe because the man in question was also on the edge of violence. First, he chatted with the patient, and in no time, they were the best of mates. This went on for about an hour until the charge nurse suggested they have something to eat – Asylum Duff! The food was good at High Royds, but the food was traditional English and heavy with old-fashioned puddings like Spotted Dick. A plate-load of a heavy suet pudding was brought in (known in the hospital as Asylum Duff and made for this very purpose), and they ate together. The charge nurse encouraged, and the patient agreed, on seconds, which he devoured. This was followed by thirds! The charge nurse himself, of course, only had a very small portion. He knew that, however manic you are, three large portions of Asylum Duff would calm even the wildest patient. Very soon, treatment was accepted and order restored. Goodness knows what they do now!

CREATURES GREAT AND SMALL

HUMAN BEINGS DO NOT EXIST in isolation. We are surrounded by flora and fauna, and since we are constantly exposed to animals, a superficial knowledge about them is useful to the family doctor. I would never go to Crickett's Cross without a tick remover, for instance. But sometimes, it is on the edge.

One day, only a few years ago, when I was a locum, a lady came in with a highly inflamed gathering on her leg, which looked like a severe reaction to a bite. The worst we were used to seeing was the huge blisters of the Blandford fly, but this was not one of those, and in any case, they were supposed to be wiped out or controlled at least. *"I have been bitten by a spider,"* she said. *"A spider!"* I responded. I do not like spiders. I've never understood why people are so forgiving of them. Apart from the fact that they scare us rigid, they show no mercy to their prey. They paralyse them, save them for later, eat them in parts and, often, the females devour their mates. Maybe, being a male, I am more sensitive to that bit. And despite their famous fly killing ability, I have never noticed a shortage of flies. *"Yes,"* she said, *"it was a false widow spider."* I immediately told her that I had never heard of a false widow and wondered how she knew. *"It was definitely a false widow,"* she said, *"because I have brought it with me, and here it is!"* Thereupon, she took out a small Kilner jar with the angriest spider I had ever seen, and I had seen a few angry spiders in Kenya. It had a large black body, relatively short legs and was very active. I recoiled and questioned the security of the jar but was reassured. The false widow is not poisonous, but some people react badly to it, and she was one. She then explained that they were all over the house, which begged the question of why she did not evict them. The reason, you may have guessed, was that she did not believe in killing spiders!

At the other end of the scale was an incident at a local farm. We still had some farms in the area, and one had a manor house and was rather stylish. The whole family were patients of mine and the lady of the house needed a home visit for a chest infection. After attending to her in the upstairs bedroom, my gaze drifted out of the window into the misty fields. I blinked. There were three large brown shapes about fifty yards away in the mist. *"For a moment,"* I said, *"I could have sworn there were some bison* in the field." "Yes,"* said the husband, *"there are three."* Evidently, there was a herd in Dorset, and because of the foot and mouth disease amongst cattle, some of the local farmers had been trying them. *"Terrible job to contain them,"* said Theo, *"they go through anything. And the vet is scared stiff of them. Won't go anywhere near them. By the way, we need to get someone to take blood for brucellosis; you wouldn't care to have a go?"* I certainly did not care to have a go! I was not going anywhere near them. In the end, they proved too much for my patients, and they had to be returned to the herd – but not before one of them had had a calf.

(*Please don't ask me the difference between a buffalo and a bison. Answer: you can't wash your hands in a buffalo!)

THE PATIENTS

I used to attend a history conference in America every year. One day, I was with some American doctors and told them about my patients. They listened spellbound. Then, one of them said, "my God, who are these people!"

OLD SAM – YOUNG SAM

O LD SAM WAS A SMALL man with a comical round face, except that there was nothing comical about him. He had started seeing me with one problem after another shortly after I had arrived. He was always anxious, a real hypochondriac. He had what is known as essential tremor. It is a coarse shake that tends to run in families and is aggravated by stress and relieved by alcohol, which he did not drink. So, he always presented himself as a shaking, nervous old man with a face full of wrinkles despite his strong-looking frame. Luckily, the retiring partner was still present, whose patients I had taken over to talk to. Dr Limbery confirmed his hypochondria but whilst Sam came to us, it was just as a backup. His main source of help was from a herbalist who he paid to visit him. We Doctors were free and, thus, not worth much. One day, I challenged him on this. He always complained of indigestion and my remedies never helped. He revealed that the herbalist would prescribe various ingredients that he would put together and give him. I asked to see them and, one day, he produced a folded white paper that contained a white powder – no name, no instructions, just an anonymous white powder. It occurred to me that the powder may have been aspirin, which would explain why Sam gained relief whilst, at the same time, suffered from continuous indigestion. I shared my suspicions with him, but there was not much else to be done, and so, we trundled on together. One day, Sam decided to forestall the grim reaper and take matters into his own hands. He hanged himself from the apple tree in his front garden, which was clearly visible from the main road when I had made the last visit to him. He was in his eighties, but as far as I could see, he had no physical illnesses. Thereafter, when driving past his old place, I always looked at the great apple tree in case he was still there. It was cut down shortly after.

When Young Sam walked in months later – a taller man in his sixties but, otherwise, like another pea in the pod – it was quite a déjà vu moment. Character-wise, they were like chalk and cheese. Young Sam was happy and confident and nearly always smiling. Clearly, Old Sam, his father, had only passed on his physical characteristics to his son. I loved chatting with him, and we did it often. It always ended with him telling me that I had the rest of the day to myself. He must have known I had the evening surgery to deal with, but it was his joke.

He had been a paratrooper during the war and was dropped on the relieving mission at Arnhem. The eleven in his squad crossed a river, but only four made it to the other side. That was the only time I ever saw him sad; it was while telling that story. The rest of the time, there was a huge grin on his face. When he returned from the war, he got married, and he and his wife put all they had on the table; it came up to 9d. After that, he and his wife worked every day, and whenever he could, he bought land. After the war, there was no money, and land was cheap in East Dorset, though it was not very good land. Scrub, pines and travellers mostly. But times changed, and in the late 70s, it was decided that an industrial estate would be built there. Some, by no means all, of Tom's land was compulsorily purchased. In compensation, the council gave him six and a half million pounds. What did he want with money? Nothing really. Years later, they gave him another three and a half million for a bit more. He still had plenty of land and wanted only one thing for it – he wanted it to lie untouched during his lifetime. After our conversations, he often chatted with my amazing secretary, Janice. In his eighties, he confided to her that he had never seen his wife naked. His wife, by that time, was no oil painting and suffered from dementia, so I suppose he never did.

PARKES

ANNIE WAS A WONDERFUL LADY. I think she died when she was ninety-three, but she was full of mischief whenever I spoke to her. She loved relating times of her girlhood in Portsmouth, where she worked cleaning the public toilets. To pass the time, they would wait for a passing tram and, with their long mop handles, knock the bowler hats off the gentlemen's heads, preferably without them knowing why, and watch them look back as they disappear down the street, confused as to where their hats had gone. She had lost a child when it was just three. I was able to talk to her about grief. Did it fade? Did it get better? No, she said, it never gets any less, but you don't think about it as often. I found it so helpful. In grief, the bereaved, whilst suffering in their own grief terribly, don't want to think that a time may come when their loved ones are forgotten. The pain is just as awful, but you don't think about it so often.

One day, she called me to see her husband, whom I had rarely seen. He had a chest infection, and thus, I had to examine his chest. We were alone, but he was reluctant to take his shirt off. I insisted and he slowly unbuttoned his shirt. There, hanging from his chest down to the umbilicus was a sac of something about the size of a baseball. With his permission, I felt it. There were convoluted veins on the outside and inside were what felt like bones and cartilage. I must have been the first person after his mother who had felt this. He was never without a shirt. His wife had never seen him without a shirt. This sac, quite large and difficult to hide, was the remains of a lost twin or what may have been meant to be a twin. I asked him if he would like it removed but he did not. He lived and died with this strange collection through his childhood, adolescence and marriage to an old age. Annie had never questioned it.

THE REVEREND

P OSSIBLY THE STRANGEST COUPLE I had ever seen was the Reverend Buckfast and his wife. He always wore a dog collar, spoke 'very far back' and had definitely taken holy orders, but to my knowledge, had never been a vicar, pastor or any official in any church – Protestant or Roman Catholic. But he wore a dog collar and looked like a vicar and his loyal and skeletal wife added to the picture of reassurance and piety. He was tall, good-looking and had plenty of dark hair, which my secretaries told me was dyed. Initially, he had a falling out with my receptionist at the time, who, wonderful lady that she was, was the archetypal dragon. In this respect, she was entirely untrained and a natural. The reverend told me later that it was at that moment that he had "decided to love her." Needless to say, this was the last response my receptionist wanted, and it drove her mad. I have no doubt that he used this fine ideal of "loving thine enemy" as a weapon very effectively, albeit harmlessly.

Looking honest and reassuring was seen by the reverend as an edge to be used. He came down to the town and used this quality to buy and sell property. Please believe me when I say that he did nothing dishonest ever, but he was able to use his shrewdness to great financial advantage. He would look at a property and target the ones difficult to sell. He would then offer to take it off their hands at a reduced price, say 5–10K lower. Meanwhile, he and his wife, and she was just as sharp, would have divined the reason it was not selling. Often it was very simple: a coat of paint, a new drive, a hedge removed – just minor cosmetics. Then, he would sell it at his leisure for 10–20K more. Everybody was happy. Another money-spinner was to make icons for the Russian Orthodox church. He would acquire pieces of wood, get pictures of various Saints, glue them, varnish them and sand them until an attractive icon had been made. He would then drive a batch or send a batch to his various contacts abroad. He was always sure to add the name – Reverend Buckfast – to the icons so that they would be reassured that they came from a religious source. Another wheeze was to go to church fairs and buy old books for prices as low as £1. Many books were almost given away. He would then sell them for a few pounds more. Small beer, perhaps, but a profit that is tax-free of 300–500%! And then, when he had accumulated a few thousand pounds, he would give it to a charity of his choice. So, his life went on. He fascinated me because I had never met anyone like him and his wife before and also had never met a person so in command of his life.

Alas, nothing goes on forever and nor did they. The terribly thin wife, who had never come to me as a patient, was clearly abnormally thin. She declined investigation, and nothing could be found on examination, apart from her low BMI. But eventually, I persuaded her to have a barium meal, which was the least unpleasant investigation we could do and the only one acceptable to her. The result was extraordinary. The pylorus, the outlet to the stomach, appeared to be a dead end. Nothing went past her stomach! The stomach was absorbing anything she was eating, if indeed she was eating at all. The rest of her gut was redundant. No counselling on my part changed their view that there was nothing to be done, and her condition slowly went downhill, and she died. Why they took this course, I often wonder. Sometimes, you can know people for years only to realise that you didn't know them at all.

The reverend, of course, was desolate, and he too declined slowly. Living alone was hard for him, but he had money. He asked me if I could find him a home help of some sort. I knew that there were several needy women in the area and mentioned it to one of them one day. She was delighted. I reassured her that he was a fine, elderly gentleman and would be a good and generous employer. I brought them together and got on with my life and work. A few weeks later, the lady came in angry and hurt. *"Did you know what he wanted?"* she asked angrily. Apparently, I did not. I had no idea and was embarrassed and mortified when she told me. I had no idea that his slender, wrinkled wife had, for all their married life, masturbated him to an orgasm every morning in bed and the reverend expected his home help to do the same! With the best will in the world, I had put together what I thought was a reasonable and sensible arrangement, only to find that I had been undone by something I could never have imagined. To say I apologised and grovelled might be an understatement. Even now, it bewilders me.

After a few years, he moved to a nursing home. He declined seriously with no particular pathology. One day, I wheeled his chair out of his room and went down by the lift until we were outside in the garden. *"What can you see up there,"* I asked. *"What is that yellow thing; what is all that blue stuff; what are those yellow flowers with the trumpet petals?"* It was, in fact, a glorious day in March, with blue skies and sunshine, and the daffodils were out. To my relief, he got the message and began to live again and did so for many years.

I knew from his comments that he was fairly well off. *"Have you made a will,"* I asked one day. He had not but promised he would when I pointedly asked him if he intended to leave it to the inland revenue! After some encouragement from me, he eventually drafted a will. After he died, I found out, triggered because some relatives, previously unmentioned, came out of the woodwork as they often do, he had made a new will every month for the previous thirteen months! Each month, a new charity was chosen, and the lucky final beneficiary turned out the be the occupational therapy department at a local hospital. I imagine it was swallowed up by the NHS. I never heard of any good coming from his donation after all his hard, if unconventional, work.

THE RAVEN

I'VE BEEN TOLD THAT MORE than 400 people are homeless in Bournemouth. By contrast, when I had lived there as a boy, there was one tramp! When I had practised in East Dorset, I had heard of one named Tom Shearing. Tom did not walk; he had a bike. He was black from head to foot with dirt and grime and cycled all over Dorset, picking things up and placing them in the front basket of his bike. It might be a screw, motor parts, food from the supermarkets, anything. It was said that during the war, he was quite useful as, if one was short of something, Tom might have one. Because he was black and ravens were believed to pinch things (should it have been a jackdaw), he was nicknamed the Raven. He was a patient I had inherited from the outgoing partner. When he came to see me, he was always sent in last because of the smell. He was ammoniacal in the extreme, but there was a powerful musty smell as well. My room was still barely fit to enter in the afternoon if Tom had been there in the morning. Nowadays, all doctors have to recite at their appraisals that they will treat patients with respect. We managed to do it without instruction in those days, and I always treated Tom with respect. On one occasion, after I had carefully treated a skin abscess, he said *"You're a gentleman."* I glowed. Then, he added, *"Not like the old doctor. He lanced my boil with his penknife! Just took it out and cut it."* Later, I mentioned it to Jock. *"Yes, he probably did, but he did it with his private patients as well!"*

I suppose now that Tom might have had some sort of autistic spectrum disorder. His talk was forced and verbose. His descriptions of every event were detailed: he would add how the sky looked and the weather at the time. He described Lawrence of Arabia's bike in intense detail from when he had met him in the thirties. I assume they were all accurate. He lived under some corrugated iron down Barrack road. I was never sure how old he was or what family he came from, but he survived, and there was a place for him in the world, unlike those homeless in Bournemouth.

One day, he arrived with quite serious leg ulcers. It was clear after a few weeks that no progress was being made, and so, I admitted him to Poole Hospital. He went without persuasion. His own agenda perhaps? A great friend of mine, Ray Matthews, was a charge nurse there, and we talked regularly. It turned out that no matter how many times they bathed and scrubbed Tom, they could never get rid of the whole smell. The ammonia went soon after admission, but the mustiness never left. It was probably just him after all those years. As the weeks passed, they wanted to discharge Tom, but he became reluctant. Tom was a survivor and adaptable. He was always seen in a wheelchair and used it to visit all parts of the hospital. They hid his wheelchair, but Tom found another. Eventually, all the wheelchairs in Poole Hospital were impounded and locked up. The next day, Tom was seen wheeling himself around in a wheelchair! The genius of acquisition which had allowed him to survive a lifetime was still intact. They discharged him in the end to a home in Clayford, where he had lived in comfort until he had died. I am sure he had kept acquiring bits to the end.

A BULL IN A FIELD AND CROSSDRESSING

S TAN HAD LIVED IN THE middle of a field with his horses. He had never looked old but neither had he ever looked as though he had been young. He just was – red-faced and smiling. He hated going to the doctor's, so I am not sure how he came to me, but I think it was because he was short of breath. He kept a load of his own horses and kept them for others as well, and he had a stream of young ladies to help him for probably nothing but the enjoyment of being with horses. Girls seem to fall in love with horses in a way that boys never do. Anyway, it all seemed to work out, but as time went on, it was clear that he had experienced a degree of heart failure, and I referred him for further evaluation. To say he was reluctant would be an understatement, but my persuasion of possible benefits eventually worked. We were in an age when medical interventions, especially cardiac, were coming thick and fast and making a huge difference. The cardiologist, who was a friend of mine, said that Stan had walked through the door and announced that he would rather face a bull in a field than be where he was then. The cardiologist suffered from the same problem I had been accused of – being blunt but good! But he listened and realised that Stan was a horseman. He, the cardiologist, had two horses. After that, they got on like a house on fire, and there were many subsequent consultations. Time passed, as it does, and Stan got to the end of the road. I was talking to my buddies in the pub one night and mentioned Stan or vice versa. Did I know he had parties up at his shack with all his girls? I did not. Did I know that they all danced together and Stan wore a dress as well and was one of the girls? Well, I didn't know that either. Being a family doctor means that you get to know your patients in a way that others don't, but as the sermon from Beyond the Fringe about the sardine tin, there is always a bit of sardine you miss!

GONE FISHIN

T OM WAS A CHARACTER. A retired builder, he enjoyed retirement and fishing in particular. He was always jolly and in good health, but his wife had asthma and bronchitis and was frail. I often had to visit and sometimes he was there and other times he was not. One morning, a desperate call was put through to me. Tom said his wife was very breathless, worse than usual, and he asked if I could come around soon. It was only a mile and I did. No one answered the door, so I walked in. His wife was gasping her last breaths. *"Where is Tom?"* I asked, horrified that he was not there and had apparently left her. She could barely breathe let alone talk, but as I desperately called for the ambulance, I could just hear, *"gone fishin."* Those were her last words. I asked Tom much later why he had left his wife to go fishing, but he never seemed to understand the question. He lived to be well over a hundred and had several girlfriends.

LEARNING QUICKLY

C ORBIN HAD BEEN ONE OF my first patients. He was thin, old-looking and when he eventually died he was only aged fifty-two. *"Those pills you gave me, Doctor, were the best I have ever had. Much better than anything the old doctor gave me."* This was his opening gambit. We learned that patients would open their conversation like a chess game, and we analysed it carefully. Never oppose an opening gambit however unacceptable. For instance, *"can I have more Thyroxine to lose weight?"* or *"Can I have some iron tablets to help my depression?"* Clearly, there is more to depression than iron tablets, but we now know that low iron, even with a normal blood count, can make people tired; so, maybe there was something to it. However, this opening gambit made me glow. The old doctor was well-respected, and I was a young colt, and here was this man comparing me favourably to the old master. He had widespread osteoarthritis and the tablets, Indomethacin, had freed him up for the first time in ages. I continued to glow until he said, *"but I can't take them!"* He explained that they had given him indigestion and had to be stopped. I was deflated, but just before I recovered from it, a document was slid in front of me. *"Would you sign this, Doctor?"* Of course, I would. It was the rescuer in the persecutor-victim-rescuer triangle. Basically, the patient challenges the doctor with something, such as *"why am I not better?"* The patient is now the persecutor and the doctor the victim. How can the doctor respond? He responds by finding a rescuer, which turns him into the persecutor and the patient the victim. *"Have you stopped smoking yet?"* Hopefully, the patient has not stopped smoking, and the doctor has been rescued! Corbin was trying this on me having had no training whatsoever. He was a natural.

Thus, I found myself signing a document that might entitle him to a free TV licence. I did not mind. I was watching; I was learning, and I kept on learning. On another occasion, that is what made me do a home visit to adjudicate between rising damp and condensation. The lady in question insisted it was rising damp and, thus, the council's responsibility, and the council said it was condensation and hers.

I learnt, read and learnt. The worst opening gambit is the one that shuts all the doors. For instance, hay fever is a seasonal, debilitating problem. The solution is avoidance, antihistamines, eye drops or nasal sprays. So, when the patient presents themself with this opener, *"I have hay fever again, Doctor. But I can't avoid it as I live next to a field; antihistamines make me drowsy; eye drops sting and nasal sprays make my nose bleed!"*, for the doctor, all the doors have been closed, and there is nowhere to go. But I learnt that there are seven possible ways out, the last of which, and I am always tempted by it, is to announce that you have already had a dreadful day and throw a tantrum! This could be the rescuer, but I have never dared to try it. I had experienced failure early on when I was called to an old lady who lived above a wonderful hardware store, which is now no longer there. She, clearly the matriarch, was in bed surrounded by her large middle-aged family. They clearly took themselves very seriously. Her problem was widespread arthritis and she announced that, *"pain killers were no good as they made her drowsy and constipated; anti-inflammatories gave her indigestion; all the operations had failed; physiotherapy was too painful,"* and a load of other things I cannot remember. All the doors were closed, and I had nowhere to go. To be fair, at that stage in my career, I should not have been asked to see her. I inquired what it was she and the family expected me to do. The next day, a load of NHS cards was on the desk from the whole family who wanted to change to someone else. But patients were signing on in droves, and I was learning. Later, I would have handled things differently.

IDLE MEN

E VER SINCE I STOPPED BEING a youth, I have been a man and for the first part of my life, was quite happy with this state. But after a decade in practice and learning more about the human state, I began to lose confidence. Men – this is not universal, of course – can be incredibly selfish. Some men can also be incredibly idle. So idle were some that I formulated a league table of idle men. They only existed thanks to some selfless women who, apparently willingly, sacrificed their lives for those men whose only resolution seemed to be idle. At the top of the league was Bert Holberton. He had eventually taken to his bed with no apparent physical or mental reason. His wife had waited on him hand and foot and even a bit more than that! She would wheel a commode into the bedroom so that he did not face the inconvenience of walking to the bathroom. His wife asked me to counsel him on these matters, but he told me that wives were there for what their husbands wanted, and he had no intention of changing. His wife colluded. She was a nurse and had had two fine daughters, a policewoman and another nurse. They did not like the situation, but they also colluded.

Bill was almost in the same mode. I remember visiting him and watching his wife struggle with a huge bucket of coke brought in from the outside. I sympathised that he could not do this as he was ill. I was told that his wife always brought the coke in because that is what wives do. Bill was a bar cellarman at the nearby pub and had no problems shifting 18- to 24-gallon casks around. There are many other examples, but they manifested themselves with the advent of Viagra. There was a time when the only recommendation from a doctor for a man with erectile dysfunction (ED) would be an electric toothbrush and a shoehorn! Without meaningful treatment, there was not much else to offer. When Viagra came on the market, the whole ED issue became frontline medicine and became serious when research showed that after the onset of ED, a cardiac event may occur after three years. In other words, ED was now a prodromal marker for heart disease. But not all men wanted Viagra for complications of their diabetes or prostate problems; they wanted to boost their waning abilities. No problem there. But what if the man's partner had begged you not to prescribe? Divided loyalties required careful management. Especially if the man was known for abusing his position.

There is a twist in the tale with Viagra. Many people think that it increases their libido, but it does not. It maintains an erection by inhibiting the destruction of the hormone that dilates penile vessels. Desire and titillation have to start the process for the Viagra to enhance it. This is where the idleness came in. What occurs in the dinner queue when seventeen does not behave in quite the same way when fifty-seven and so on. But many men behave as though it should and make no dispensation to their age. They will wine and dine with a lady, have three or four pints and curry or a three-course meal, and thus furnished with food and drink, expect to be able to function as they used to. They then take Viagra and guess what, it doesn't work! Apart from the fact that there is a lot more to foreplay than food and drink, I have to explain basic physiology, which could be explained as basic plumbing. If the average man has seven to eight pints of circulating blood with two to three swishing around the lungs at any given moment to be oxygenated, that leaves five to six pints for the rest of the body. If the man then has a large meal, two pints will be diverted to the splanchnic vessels for digestion, thus leaving three to four pints for the whole of the rest of the body. It is an accepted fact that the average man does not have enough blood to supply both his brain and erect his penis at the same time, which explains, according to women, a lot about male behaviour. But likewise, it is not easy to supply the erect penis, the brain and the gut at the same time. In other words, and I will paraphrase mildly, if you are going to eat, eat, and if you are going to have sex, have sex, but not both at the same time. If you are going to make love to a woman, make that the priority! So, many of the men I referred to decided that the food and drink were the priority and any more was too much trouble!

Please forgive a moment's digression because erectile dysfunctions are not always what one would imagine. Once an old chap had hypertension, and I had given him a long-acting water tablet to be taken in the morning. It is a mild and relatively harmless way of treating mild hypertension. Alas, it must have been a very long action for him because it was still working at night and filling his bladder with the surprise side effect of an unwanted erection! He sat in front of me with that indignant look country folk are good at throwing and berated me, *"I wake up and there it is. And at my age, I've no use for it!"*

On another occasion, at the end of morning surgery, I met an exhausted-looking man called Morgan. During the war, he had been hailed as a hero but quite mistakenly, he explained. When the shells started landing at Alamein, he jumped in his lorry and cleared off as fast as he could. As he drove, he kept on being stopped by injured men, whom he took on board. When he arrived back, he was lauded as the saviour of the injured whereas he was desperately trying to save his own skin. It was he who, tired and drained, was seated in front of me. He had recently been presented with depression with all the classical symptoms and standard sleep disturbances and had warranted an anti-depressant. That night, he and his wife had decided to make love. One of the symptoms of depression is supposed to be the loss of libido, which never seemed to be the case in East Dorset. One of the side effects of anti-depressants is delayed ejaculation. Both he and his wife had felt that sex was not complete without male ejaculation, so they had carried on and on until the state of exhaustion had overcome resolution and required an angry consultation the next day!

...AND FRUSTRATED WOMEN

I ALWAYS WENT TO MEET MY patients in the waiting room. My partners preferred to use the tannoy, but I always felt that it discriminated against handicapped people who might not hear properly despite our loop system or because of infirmity or other factors. Also, I liked the exercise, and I liked to know what was going on. One comfortable middle-aged lady took advantage of it. She would jump up and announce to the waiting room that she had a bone to pick with me and, equally suddenly, would come over, declare that she had forgiven me and hug me! I would accept it. What I did not know as the years went on was that that was all the physical contact she had ever had with a man. Her first husband had died, and in widowhood, she had wanted a man. She was married again to a very pleasant, avuncular man but was horrified to find that there would be no physical contact. Not just sex – nothing. No hugs, no touching, nothing. For some people, probably most people, that is a diabolical form of sensory deprivation, and there was nothing she could do about it – apart from taking advantage of me. I found many women frustrated like that. Early on, a lady of fifty-two, would come in and ask for her Mogadon. Mogadon or nitrazepam is a benzodiazepine used to help induce sleep. It would be considered wrong now, but no doubt, many of the things we consider right now will be considered wrong in the future. One might ask why so much is wrong if we have so much right now! Anyway, we did prescribe such drugs but, of course, I asked her why she needed them. She too had a husband who declined physical contact. She confided that each night, she would take her two capsules and grip the sides of the bed until she went to sleep. How awful for her. Was a late-night cuddle too much for her husband? Apparently, it was. He had no impediment, as far as I knew. Decades later, I saw her in a nursing home. She was dementing. I reflected on all those frustrating years she had endured. She didn't deserve it.

In this enlightened age of LBGTQ, it is hard to remember that when I had started my practice, homosexuality was a criminal offence. It existed, of course, but closeted. One coping strategy to mask the issue was for the homosexual male to hide behind the cover of marriage. There were several such marriages amongst my patients. Those poor women, unknowing, perhaps, or knowing and believing they could change their man, were then condemned to a sexless, contactless, barren existence. The ones I knew faced such a life for the rest of their marriage. They must have married innocently, looking forward to physicality, children and all that marriage can bring, only to endure physical abnegation for life. My heart bled for them.

NO BLUE LIGHT

━━

E NGLISH PEOPLE, IN GENERAL, AND Dorset folk, in particular, are quiet and modest. Being forceful is referred to as "showing yourself up." Often, foreigners, who have always fought for all they have, misinterpret this and take advantage of it. One amusing example of reticence is when Mr Copeland, aged eighty, came in and confided in me that he had a bit of chest pain. There were no physical signs, so I said we would need to take an ECG. A few minutes later, I was explaining to him that he was having a heart attack and needed to go to the hospital immediately. *"No blue light,"* he responded quietly, *"I don't want a blue light and people talking."* Amazing. He was having a heart attack and knew exactly what that meant but did not want a blue light ambulance! As it happens, this presented a problem for me. When calling for an ambulance, they have their own protocols. If you want an ambulance pronto, it has to be 'blue light.' Anything else takes four hours or, if less of a priority, much longer. The ambulance control can be less than helpful at times. We were all under pressure. The worst experience I had was when I was called to a man who had been seen by two of my colleagues already. As I walked through the bedroom door, I could see the poor chap had a fractured neck of femur and a bladder up to his umbilicus! He had urinary retention, having fallen and broken his hip. I called an ambulance and demanded it to be as quick as possible. Because I had not specifically mentioned the 'blue light,' the jobsworth at the other end put him on a four-hour wait. I complained on behalf of the patient, but health service complaint procedures are designed to make you lose the will to live.

Therefore, I was now begging for a blue light ambulance that did not flash its blue lights! When it arrived, I had a quiet word with the ambulance men who smiled and understood. They were also Dorset people.

ALADDIN'S CAVE

HOWARD ANDREWS IRRITATED ME; THERE was no doubt about it. It did not matter whether you asked him an open or a closed question, his answer was protracted, flowery, circumlocuitous and went around the houses. In a busy surgery, he was a pain. He had a slight accent, and he revealed that he was, in fact, Polish. I knew all about the role Poles played during WW2 and how they fought well, made great fighter pilots and started the enigma code-cracking. I had a trainee doctor at the time who was the son of such a Polish family and was proud of his background. He was disapproving though of Poles who changed their names. Real Poles, he contended, should have names that read like the bottom line of the optician's eye chart.

Howard certainly had physical complaints, with only one kidney, and I was usually busy, but on one particular day, he didn't have much, and I had spare time. I took the opportunity to satiate my curiosity. *"Howard, why did you change your name?"* He looked at me thoughtfully and, in his soft accent, began, *"When I was a boy in Poland, we holidayed in Ukraine."* Here we go, I thought, round the houses again or, in this case, around Eastern Europe! He continued with his story and explained that when the war had started, he was only fifteen but still managed to lie about his age and join the army. They were eventually heavily beaten in a three-week campaign in the end. He had managed to survive and, being familiar with Ukraine, decided to go there and pretend to be a Ukrainian peasant boy since he knew the language. As the years went by and he heard of the stand-in Warsaw, he returned and took up fighting again. They fought in the streets and the sewers, but eventually, seeing the hopelessness of the situation, he got out. He worked his way across Europe and was able to surrender to American forces who interned him in France. It was there, in France, that he had learnt English. He could speak French, and it was from the French-speaking background that he learnt his English. That was why his English was so flowery. I remembered my cycling days when I had read French cycling magazines. They could spend a whole page talking about Jacques Anquetil's legs!

He had then been transferred to England, worked where he could, met a girl, got married and the rest, as they say, is history. This tale, of which I have related a small part, was mesmerising. This quiet, modest man was living the history of the Polish struggle and survival. It took me a while to take it in, when suddenly I remembered, *"But Howard, the question I asked was why did you change your name?" "Oh," he said, "in view of what had happened, I thought my name was the least of my problems!"* It wasn't really an answer, but at least it was brief.

Patients and people are like Aladdin's cave. When you say the magic words, jewels are revealed – hidden most of the time but priceless when found.

TRAINING

AFTER ABOUT FIVE YEARS IN General Practice, I had been approached to start training GPs. I thought it was too soon, but the Associate had seen something in me. I had given a few talks and we had a spare surgery room available for a Trainee GP. He must have really seen something because I went on training without a break for the next thirty years! I was very lucky with my trainees, and training became a major part of my life. I never had any breaks for the first six weeks of the year until the new doctor had become functional and confident in the practice. My first trainee was, in fact, a year older than me and had left paediatrics. It was the blind leading the blind, but it was great fun. I realised that the best way to learn was to teach others, and as medical knowledge was expanding so fast, I always had a head start. My whole year revolved around the advent of the new trainee. The concept of a year's training in GP had just begun, stimulated locally by Dr George Swift. This vocational training was to be based on the apprenticeship system, and although apprenticeship is one of the few validated methods of teaching, there was no assessment. Therefore, it depended on the quality of the trainer, who could transmit their bad habits as well as good. Apprenticeship was ideal for a "jack of all trades," which was what we were. It gave the new doctor confidence and was alright if – and this was the big if – the future job would be the same as the old.

Apart from George Swift, there were many inspiring leaders. John Fry from Beckenham in Kent had written something about every patient he had ever seen from 1943 and had compiled a book on the natural history of common diseases. Today, no disease has not been interfered with by modern medicine, so often their natural history is not known. The classic example is Prostate cancer. I half the cases the cancer is dangerous and in half it is benign. Which half is the patient in? Thus, millions of men who did not need it were vigorously treated for prostate cancer.

Michael Balint made us reflect deeply on the doctor–patient relationship and our power in the healing process. We became aware of the orientation of our work. Disease-orientated medicine focused on the disease rather than the patient. James Willis wrote *The Paradox of Progress*, which explained that the more we focus on diseases, the more we discard other factors. Our disease-oriented approach facilitates the exclusion of knowledge, and this is the exact opposite of what a 'jack of all trades' needs in the environment he or she works in. We became aware of the technical–healing spectrum; a patient can have technically good treatment but may not feel or get better. I related elsewhere about a man who had a pacemaker put in quickly and efficiently, but he needed his doctor to explain that he would no longer fall and could join the land of the living. We learned of the doctor–patient contract. We knew that the best medicine was holistic, and the only true holistic medicine was our family medicine because it embraced the parameter of time. No other medicine does this; they are clinic medicine.

In 1987, Roger Neighbour published *The Inner Consultation*, which helped us to reflect on and understand the consultation. It became the bible of the trainee but, like all progressions, had an unforeseen casualty. Prior to this, we had used consultation analysis, which did exactly what it said – it analysed the consultation. Consultations have a beginning, a middle and an end. We learned never to reject the opening gambit and we became masters of terminating the consultation, something that young doctors and nurses find the hardest to do. We were also aware of the anatomy of the middle of the consultation and how to use it. *The Inner Consultation* provided insight, but the mechanics of getting through the consultation tended to be lost.

A part of the training was using videos. We saw ourselves for the first time! That was a shock and was only needed once! But we asked ourselves what had gone well and what had gone not so well. We asked ourselves what could be done differently. We discussed if there was a learning need and how it could be addressed.

Apprenticeship had no assessment, and this was clearly a problem;

so, we began formative assessments. It was a constructive way of learning and assessing learning needs. The trainer and trainee formulated mutual statements of teaching.

The next stage was a sort of test, which was called Summative Assessment. It was initially a test to eliminate the 2% of doctors who were a danger to the public and themselves. But it was quickly realised that you could not set a test that 98% of the candidates would pass! So, the test was tightened up and eventually absorbed by the Royal College of GPs. All this sounds like progress, but as G. K. Chesterton observed, not all progress is in the right direction. Apart from the fact that the act of measuring something alters it, there were changes. The first thing to go was the video and, with it, the observation of the doctor examining the patient. This was now left for the trainer to do as the examination was lost as part of the consultation and became an isolated event to be prepared for. To explain in simple terms, while on the video one might observe that the doctor failed to examine the chest of a breathless person properly, that would not be the case if the doctor was instructed to examine a chest while being observed. In 2004, the video was replaced by a 'simulated surgery' or Clinical Skills Assessment. It was considered to be better because it was thought that some trainees might cherry-pick their patients and their conditions, and also, some trainees said they could not make videos. But CSA does not include examination, which is still a flaw for the reason I stated above. The biggest change occurred in the relationship between the trainer and the trainee. The trainer was no longer obliged to teach; the trainee was obliged to pass the test! The obligation was now firmly on the trainee who jumped through the hoops or failed. The tests altered the training and resulted in some doctors wanting to extend their training to learn basic procedures. The video was dropped completely, and a brilliant learning tool was replaced by a grid of boxes to be filled in. The process of assessment took away the power of the video to do things differently and to change ourselves. The habit of the modern doctor in spending the consultation looking into a screen would have been cruelly exposed as he looked at himself!

To be fair, bad doctors now had difficulty slipping through the net, and there was quality control. The excellent probably excelled anyway.

The three big changes that altered training was the advent of clinical governance in 1990, NICE guidelines in 2000 and the Quality Outcomes Framework in 2004. I do not wish to examine all these processes, which were very useful to young doctors, but I recommend them to those who suffer from insomnia. However, we came to realise that the word "guideline" in fact meant "written on tablets of stone." They began to shackle the thoughtful GP and were invasively prescriptive. They were unhelpful to the "jack of all trades." QOF, which I mentioned earlier, was target driven, population-based, disease orientated and driven by protocol rather than guidelines. As I hinted at earlier, QOF was good for those included, but not so good for those outside the targets and non-existent for the excluded! It medicalised a vast number of people at a great expense with uncertain outcomes. It exhibited a touching faith in the current guidelines and a blind spot to its shortcomings. In many ways, the NICE guidelines and clinical governance were ways of hiding the downward pressure of prescribing and referral.

We began training the new GP with high hopes. We had detached ourselves from the doctor-orientated approach where doctors controlled the consultation; we detached ourselves from disease-orientated medicine driven by specialists. We developed ways to train them for patient-sensitive and patient-orientated care. As the changes developed, we found ourselves going back to the disease-orientated care based on targets, controlled by NICE and QOF. Could that be why doctors spend their time staring at the screen after you waited three weeks to see them?

> To lighten the mood, I would like to quote W. H. Auden.
> Give me a doctor partridge plump
> short in the leg and broad in the rump
> an endomorph with gentle hands
> who'll never make absurd demands
> that I abandon all my vices
> or pull long faces in a crisis.
> But, with a twinkle in his eye...
> will tell me when I have to die!

Alas, this one by Marie Compton is more appropriate
today.
Give me a doctor underweight
computerised and up-to-date
the businessman who understands
accountancy and target bands
who demonstrates sincere devotion to audit and
health promotion.
But, when my outlook's for the worse...
refer me to the practice nurse!

COMPUTER

—

W E GOT OUR FIRST COMPUTER in 1982. We were one of the first fifty practices in the country to have one and it was very much our own thing. We had a computer geek named Mike who wrote his own programme. It was presented in MS-DOS, there was no Windows then, and written in a computer language called MUMPS. MUMPS is described in Wikipedia as follows:

*MUMPS ("Massachusetts General Hospital Utility Multi-Programming System"), or **M**, is a general-purpose computer programming language originally designed in 1966 for the healthcare industry. Its differentiating feature is its "built-in" database, enabling high-level access to disk storage using simple symbolic program variables and subscripted arrays; similar to the variables used by most languages to access main memory.[1]*

It continues to be used today by many large hospitals and banks to provide high-throughput transaction data processing.

Each patient was given a number based on their date of birth just as my bank does today. As the information was entered, a disease code could be ascribed to that patient, e.g., DIA for diabetes, and then, by entering DIA, all the information for all the diabetics would be presented. And it could hunt for free text! Was that brilliant or what? Of course, we could not impede the advent of Windows-based systems, but frankly, they were not as good. The NHS offered financial help, not much, and suggested a 4GB floppy disk as memory. It sounds risible now, but it fact it was risible at the time. They had no idea how much memory healthcare required and even now, because everything is retained, they still don't. The real reason we had to change was not that the new systems were better but because we were unconnected to other systems. Thirty-eight years later, there are still different systems in General Practice. Hospitals are much worse now with one system for basic consultations, another for X-Rays, another for ECGs and another for pathology. Often, the poor doctor can only get into one at a time. No wonder the patients in the emergency department have to wait so long despite all the departments working their best. Hopefully, that will have improved by the time this is published.

Progress is painful at times. Recently, while doing GP appraisals, I was shown that the doctors were given laptops to access the patients' notes anywhere. Before I had retired, I used a Blackberry to do that!

It was said in the early days of computerised records that it should be our servant and not our master. As always, it is a bit of both. But one thing that did happen was that it facilitated the control of GP by the government. They were not just our paymasters; they were our masters.

FROM OPPORTUNISTIC TO POPULATION AND THE RISE OF THE WORRIED WELL

IN THE EARLY DAYS, A patient went to the doctor when they were ill. We also took the time to review their health in general. If a man came in, say an overweight smoker, whose blood pressure turned out to be high and, perchance, had sugar in his urine, we would pile in our advice and treatment options. In this way, we would provide that man many years of quality life. QALY (quality-adjusted life-years) is a measurement of perfect health and is used to assess the benefit of advice or treatment. The man I just described may gain ten to twenty QALYs as a result of a change of course. This meant a huge difference to the individual. Conversely to the national health statistics, it meant very little. Such interventions would barely show as a hiccup in the larger assessments of health. Statisticians realised that to affect overall health statistics, a population approach was needed. So, a reduction in blood pressure of x in the whole population would mean a reduced rate of stroke in y. So it was with blood sugar, cholesterol, weight and smoking. This was good for statistics but very little good for the life of each patient and dispiriting for doctors. The worst effect was that it turned almost everyone over fifty into a patient. Patients were no longer ill; they suffered from having surrogate markers outside the most favourable ideals. Everyone began to know their total cholesterol. They did not suffer from heart disease; they suffered from cholesterol. I remember an elderly lady proudly declaring that she had cholesterol! I explained that since the cholesterol molecule was a fundamental building block of most of the body's complex molecules, it was not surprising. It is as important as bricks are to houses. Instead of seeing sick people, the GP was now manipulating these surrogate markers. This job was intended to be the role of nurses or clinics, but it never fully happened, and it was all focused through QOF. The Quality and Outcomes Framework was introduced with yet another new contract in April 2004. GPs were required to achieve hundreds of targets and received money for doing so. This, as I have said, was money taken away from them to pay for it. Year after year, it was adjusted to take in new areas or drop old ones. There are two things I must clarify. First, just in case anyone thinks I could not cope with QOF, our practice gained maximum points for every year that I was there. I take no credit as it was a fastidious partner and our staff who always reached the final few markers. Second, it definitely improved the management of a large number of patients. However, many, if not most, were patients who were not ill and at medium to low risk. It diverted a huge amount of time and effort of the practice and had one gigantic flaw. There were some patients with many morbidities who were almost too complicated to manage. These patients required very special attention and care. Believe it or not, it was possible to exclude them from the QOF. The very patients who needed the most were exempted. Nine categories of patients could be excluded, and each reason sounds perfectly reasonable on its own. But in practice, doctors just took the patients they could not cope with and reported them as an exception. Some doctors were worse than others, but I have never seen an 'exception' being challenged by the health authority.

The population approach altered Nation Health Statistics and improved the health of those with moderate or medium risk, but it diverted the GP from opportunistic screening and the seriously ill. Appointments with one's own doctor became more difficult until the concept of "one's own doctor" became a memory. One's own doctor was, in fact, busy fine-tuning the worried well because that was the way he or she earned money. There was no mileage in attending to the acutely sick. At a post-graduate meeting, I remember being told by a cardiologist that we too busy to continually visit patients with heart failure. Heart failure has a prognosis compatible with the major cancers. That is exactly what we should be doing.

There is a lovely cartoon of an old GP sitting behind his desk, pen in hand, writing his notes. A man comes in wielding an axe. He says, "Doctor, I have an uncontrollable urge to chop doctors up with an axe." The old doctor continues writing, does not look up and says,

"There's a lot of it about,

bowels alright,

how's the wife?"

It is meant to be a joke, but there is enough truth in it to provoke a chuckle. But if it happened today, a similar doctor, eyes glued to his screen, would reply,

"Did Sister take your BP,

I don't think I have your BMI,

shouldn't you be on a statin?"

Having increased the number of patients by redefining them as having a problem, naturally, people became interested in these imaginary conditions. This led to the rise of the "worried well." The rock-solid common sense of the semi-rural indigenous population was being replaced by the anxieties of the retired elderly, who now began to settle in Clayford. They aged and were reluctant to die, but they had forgotten how to live. Their bible was the Tuesday edition of the Daily Mail, which was carefully crafted to exploit their fears. They would come in clutching the relevant pages with sections marked for my opinion. Many of the articles suggested that their doctor was, in fact, trying to poison them and not help them. Whilst not denying that there might be some truth to this, I can honestly say in my case that it was accidental and not deliberate. What I really wanted was for them to start living again. Atul Gawande defines it clearly in *Being Mortal*. The concept of people who never die is not new. The bitter satirist, Jonathan Swift, was aware of them in the 19th century and wrote that Gulliver, on hearing of this race who never died but were unhappy, wished to visit them. You can find his visit to Luggnagg to see the Struldbruggs in book three, chapter ten. Unfortunately, although they did not die, they could age. One feature that rings a bell is that the younger generation began to use different words that could not be understood by the older ones. Swift's Struldbruggs were different from mine, but the point was made. Having a long life is not the same as a long experience of living.

At this point, it is pertinent to quote Aldous Huxley: "Medical science has made such tremendous progress that there is hardly a healthy human left."

Having redefined what it is to be a patient, an unintended consequence followed: doctors embraced this new 'patient' and concentrated on the surrogate markers, the guidelines and the governance. They forgot that the chief factors for good health are clean water, good food, exercise, warmth, hygiene and yes, genes. I am fortunate to have three friends who are all aged ninety-six (two of them are previous patients). They are all active and in good health. One had survived a plane crash; one had flown Spitfires during WW2, was shot down twice and endured a prison camp from which he escaped; the third is different in that, although he had flown planes, he had never crashed. They had all smoked at some stage of their lives, and they drink; in fact, when the Spitfire man came to brunch recently, he started his full English breakfast with a brandy. None of them went to the gym or ate 'healthy.' Conversely, young and middle-aged people lose their lives for no apparent reason. There is the element of luck in this that confounds the patients and doctors who think that continual fine-tuning of the surrogate markers will lead to a long and healthy life. It merely consumes the life of the patient who has forgotten how to live and the Doctor who is now married to his targets.

EQUIPMENT

T HE MOST IMPORTANT PIECES OF equipment for a doctor are indeed their eyes and ears – looking and listening. The sense of touch from one's fingertips and the sense of smell follow closely behind. The sense of taste I would exclude, although I had once tasted a lady's urine because I was so certain that she had taken her specimen from the tap for reasons known only to her! Most people would think of a stethoscope when thinking of medicine. But the otoscope, ophthalmoscope and other such devices are also useful. I have found that one of the most useful pieces of equipment is the scales and was obsessive enough to calibrate mine with a 56 lb wt. It is the simplest and easiest way to monitor fluid retention or loss in heart failure. Apart from obvious cases in thyroid disease, diabetes and cancer, a patient with depression and weight loss is far more concerning than one without.

I was very proud of my ear syringe, donated to me by my previous partner. If you could restore a person's sight, it would be classed as a miracle, but for some reason, restoring hearing by the simple act of removing whatever is blocking the ear meatus is not. Also, it is not done now very often. *"We don't do it now,"* is one of the familiar calls of the practice nurse as though that is a reason in itself. One of our local consultants sent around a request to practices asking how many ear syringes they did in a year. It was huge. Then, he asked the ENT casualties how many problems they had each year attributable to ear syringing. The answer was zero. He concluded that ear syringing was safe and effective. Can it ever be classified as an emergency procedure? One patient thought so as he told my secretary, who then fitted him in at the end of surgery. Ear syringing needs no preparation and takes minutes, so I did not mind, but I was intrigued why this was an emergency. So, he told me: one of the managing directors had dropped dead the day before and an interview for a new one was to be held at midday. He wanted the job but knew he was markedly deaf. A quick syringe and all ended happily ever after!

The equipment was mostly kept in the doctor's bag. In the days when we could call consultants out on a domiciliary visit and joke about was what they kept in their bags. It was said that a surgeon would have only one thing – a glove! A neurologist would have a patellar hammer, a psychiatrist's bag would be full of psychotropic drugs, and so on. But our bags held everything! We had pills, injections and all the scopes we could hold. I had three thermometers of the old mercurial kind – oral, rectal and low temperature. But the item we learned very early in our careers to never, ever – and I am tempted to add another ever – be without, was a glove. I always had plenty of gloves in my bag and a full pack in the car. The advent of lady doctors meant that the size of the available gloves changed from large to medium or even small, and if you weren't careful to check, you could reduce the male hand to something small and white with all the blood cut off, which would nullify proper examination.

However, the strangest and possibly most useful piece of equipment I had was a crystal ball! I daresay you may have an odd smirk at this stage because it is not possible to see the future, and there is no such thing as a crystal ball that can. So, let me explain. Imagine you are in the surgery and this patient who is facing you asks, *"Doctor, do you think I should go on holiday next week?"*

"Yes, of course, you should."

"But I am afraid of being ill again."

"Well, if you really think you are going to be ill, you should not go."

"But I have been really looking forward to it."

"In that case, you should go."

"But I am really concerned about what might happen."

"In that case, you should not go."

"But I have paid a lot of money for this holiday, and I may not get it back."

"In that case, definitely go."

Trust me, dear reader, this sort of mindless conversation can go on for ages if uninterrupted. One of the things we used to teach was how to regain control of the consultation. There are many ways, but in this case, I would have reached across my desk and brought out my crystal ball. I would then explain that we needed to see into the future, and I would intently gaze into my paperweight with bubbles in. The penny would always drop; the patient would get the message and respond with either a sigh or an apology. I must have saved days of consultation time over the years with this strategy.

Another piece of equipment I used, which was unique to me (and the fictional Dr McCoy,) was the cantilever couch. I noticed from watching Star Trek that, while our aged rheumatic patients had to clamber up on the examination couch, Captain Kirk, who was perfectly able to leap up unaided, never did so because of the slick cantilever couch used by Dr McCoy. I decided my patients should be treated with this sort of care. It took a while, but eventually, I found the right couch in three sections and used it thereafter.

PROGRESS

I N 1972, GENERAL PRACTICE WAS run by the Executive Council, one of the three branches of the National Health Service. In Dorset, it was administered by a chief executive, a finance officer and someone else! The practice was paid for the work done, and we also had modest expenses. Therefore, money came in and went out, and what was left was the profit to be divided amongst the partners. The sums were small, and the accounts were simple. 1974 saw the re-organisation of the health service and the EC became the Family Practitioner Committee. It was decided that we would purchase certain aspects of health care and would be reimbursed for them. Money began to pour in but, equally, money poured out. The accounts were not complicated, but the transactions were many, so we thought it best to appoint our own finance officer. We were lucky enough to get a retired chartered accountant, and he became a bit of a legend in the practice for his miserly care of our cash. As things became more complicated, we thought it a good idea to appoint a practice manager to oversee the processes in the practice. We employed our own practice nurse and, shortly afterwards, a secretary for her. Although the sums of money rose five- to six-fold, our profits remained the same. Likewise, the work we did remained mostly the same apart from the increasing list size due to development. The EC, which was run by three people, became the FPC with a huge department. Progress was being made, but it was difficult to see in what direction. The FPC also expanded greatly to bill us and send out corresponding remuneration. Also, the accounting bills went up, and accountants became more important in our planning. Everyone had become much busier, but as doctors, we did the same work and made the same profit!

The best appointment I had made was our practice nurse in 1974.

Four years later, we rebuilt the health centre, expanded the treatment room and gave her a secretary. She was an expensive item of labour (but worth her weight in gold), and we did not want her to answer the phone and do clerical work. She was super-efficient anyway, and the treatment room became a vital part of the practice where a lot of the action took place.

During the 80s, there was more progress. The managerial revolution was summed up in perfection by an article in the BMJ. Slowly, the administrators who had guided the health service through its early decades were retiring and being replaced by managers. It was felt that the old administrators were holding things back due to their experience (in truth their main experience was in running the health service on a shoestring). New people with no experience would be much easier to promote and 'change' was the new watchword – we were all to embrace change. The mantra of the managers was to start with a clean sheet of paper and a level playing field. The current practice was to be discarded and the problems thrown in the air, whereupon the managers would sort them before they landed. Managing was considered to be a generic skill, so it did not matter what speciality they came from; they could be trained. Thus, we had chiropodists managing the physiotherapists, the health visitors managing the district nurses and any combination you could care to think of. I don't think anyone managed the midwives but the midwives themselves. Unfortunately, the administrators had been professionals with professional values, just like the doctors, and this quality was lost.

It reminded me of Socrates description of the 'Ship of Fools' where the sailors try to pilot the vessel 'with no knowledge of the year and seasons and sky and stars and winds and whatever else belongs to the pilot's art.' Success on the 'Ship of Fools' is defined not by the skills to navigate but by the ability to persuade others that such skills are not necessary and the job can be done regardless. Change was the watch word and those who embraced it got the jobs and those who counselled hard work were derided.

By 1979, the country was in a dire state, and it was difficult to even get a light bulb changed in our health centre, but by the end of the 80s, this had all changed, and in 1990, we had a new contract and were able to re-build our health centre once more. Health promotion was the new mantra, and we were given money to do virtually any sort of health promotion we could think of. Where did this money come from? Why, out of our pockets, of course. It is worth saying a word about GP money because the NHS had now realised it had a wonderful way of controlling a speciality, who were ostensibly self-employed. The terms and conditions of service I had mentioned earlier were readable at first, but the NHS, being more powerful than the profession, realised it could change them at will. A review body worked out the total sum going into general practice and how it was divided was in the terms and conditions of service. Thus, money could be taken out or reduced and then offered back to the doctors if they did the things that the NHS had thought up for them. Like all ideas, this sounded hopeful in the beginning. Before 1990, innovation had emerged from individual doctors and practices, and some of the changes were remarkable. In my practice, the way we developed our treatment room in the 1970s and the advent of our first computer in 1982 were examples. But we were just part of a great innovative surge in general practice. The problem was that this was not universal, giving rise to inequalities. One might say that this was perfectly reasonable in independent businesses. However, it was not acceptable to the government, which felt quite rightly that the taxpaying public (this was the age of Mrs Thatcher who constantly reminded her ministers that there was no such thing as government money, only the taxpayers' money!) were entitled to equality in health care. Unfortunately, the solution was to standardise general practice in every way. Remember the law of unintended consequences? This is an example as it was good to raise the standards of poor practices, but it completely paralysed the innovation of the good practices that had developed. Good doctors stopped thinking. Worse, the doctors coming into general practice became used to this control and, in my opinion, became used to being bullied. Clinical governance became the watchword, and whilst there was much good in this, there was little room for manoeuvring. One size never fits all. There was much downward pressure on prescribing costs, which at first sight sounds perfectly right and proper. But ask yourself this question – would you go to a shop that only sold the cheapest items? The answer is that you would for some things but not for others. A second question – would you prescribe this drug to a member of your family? If you, as a doctor, cannot say that you are treating your patients exactly as you would treat your own family, you are being dishonest and not fit to practice.

COMETH A WHITE KNIGHT

C LAYFORD DID NOT HAVE MUCH to its name. It was a place people passed through. It had three distinct populations. There was the semi-rural, indigenous population, whom I had inherited from Ian Limbery. They were the people who had previously worked on the land. Some were settled itinerants, some settled travellers and some genuine settled gypsies. They seemed to have few surnames, and as time went on, I suspected they were all related to one another in some way. Indeed, through convoluted pathways, I found myself connected to one of the larger families. The second group had the retired army officers, often from the Indian army, brought in by my senior partner, Jock, who had spent his war days travelling around Bombay on an elephant with the governor. The third population was the newcomers. The land was cheap at first and the area nice; hence, new estates grew. It was a handy place being approximately equidistant from three nearby towns and three further away cities.

Though it did not have much to recommend it, it had a famous golf course, and associated with it, but not part of it, was a small but attractive hotel, the Dormy, which, in golfing terms, I believe, means you can't lose. After I had been there a few years, the long-standing manager of the Dormy, a real character, retired. He was replaced by a young man who quickly ran away with a barmaid. My remembrance is, I confess, that she was worth running away for. This was followed by another young man, who was stepping onto uncertain ground after years of stability. How would he fare?

The answer to that is he fared badly at first. After a few weeks, a man broke into the hotel one evening and badly assaulted the deputy manager. I can't remember if that was before or after a dead body was found floating in the swimming pool. The pool was in the open air in those days, but either way, it set a bad example. I was called one day because a lady had gone mad in one of the rooms and was scaring the guests and staff alike. When I went to report to the new manager, he was sitting slumped behind his desk, accompanied and supported by three staff members who were, no doubt contemplating the trinity of assaults of his deputy, the body in the pool and the psychotic lady. My initial reaction was *"This boy won't last!"*

How wrong I was.

To be fair the Hotel was flooded two weeks later and he confided to his wife that maybe the move to Clayford was a mistake. He was wrong too!

The new manager, Derek, turned out to be an extraordinary man – ebullient, confident, capable, honest and modest. He was always thinking of new ideas, especially for charities, through his beloved golf. He nurtured contacts, knew everyone and was universally liked. From my point of view and the Practice's, he was also a white knight, although I doubt if – until he read this – he knew how.

We had moved into a phase where practices could buy and use medical equipment. To this end, I had started an equipment fund to which grateful patients could contribute, and we had raised about three to four thousand pounds. The Health Authority wanted practices to modernise but effected it by making the practices earn their money by doing, frankly, stupid things. Goodness knows who came up with them. They wasted huge amounts of time, especially in practice strategy meetings. At a BMA conference in Bournemouth, they were openly described as 'destructive innovation'. Derek allowed us to ignore some of these things because we had our own money. He approached me one day and asked if we needed money for equipment. Anything was welcome, I replied. *"Would £10,000 do?"* My eyes were wide in shock. He had planned to use us as the recipient of the money he had raised at the pro/am golf tournament. He also managed to get the captain to designate us as his charity as well for another £10,000! This was big money then and fairly big now. Thus, we acquired computerised ECGs, respiratory function monitors, videos for teaching, relaxation chairs, label printers and anything and everything we wanted without having to jump through hoops for it. He did it again after a few years and on my retirement, which gave us another chance. Since I was retiring, it was up to the remaining partners. But they were not interested. The sum was £60,000!

This money gave us independence and control. Priceless.

SLOWLY DE-SKILLED

———

N OT ALL DOCTORS WANT TO do all things. So, why take away skills from those who have been using them for decades?

Minor Ops

I and my partners would perform minor operations on most weeks. We reinforced our skills with courses, and the service was cheap and convenient for the patients. The patient would present a lump or mole and, if appropriate, would be put down for the following session. It would be removed and sent to pathology. A week or so later, the patient would return for the doctor to remove the sutures, examine their work and discuss the pathology with the patient. At this point, you, the dear reader, will be wondering where anything could go wrong! Nevertheless, an edict appeared saying that a register must be kept of all the transactions. The doctor, a professionally trained person, was no longer deemed to be responsible enough to keep this register. It had to be kept by a clerk. Next, a paper appeared locally to say that GPs made too many errors, and 40% of biopsies were unsuitable. But in what way was not defined. It was outrageous nonsense, but nonetheless, GPs were forbidden from removing anything but the most innocent-looking lesions. Our patients now had to travel seven miles to the Poole dermatology department to be seen by another doctor who would make the same diagnosis. An appointment would then be made for a nurse, who was trained for this purpose, to remove the lesion – another fourteen-mile round trip. Doctors who had been competent for years were now deemed to be incompetent. Soon, the dermatology department was swamped, and the facio-maxillary unit was asked to help out. I think they were swamped as well! A first-class reliable and convenient service had just been wiped out, and for what?

In August 2018, a paper was published in the Journal of General Practice. It compiled the results from a whole-Scotland melanoma cohort in primary and secondary care. It compared those patients who had had their first cutaneous surgery done by their GP and those who had gone to a hospital. The results were as follows: "Patients in Scottish rural locations were more likely to have a melanoma excised in primary care. However, those in the rural areas did not have a significantly increased mortality (in fact, they had none at all) from melanoma. Together, these findings suggest that the current UK melanoma management guidelines could be revised to be more realistic by recognising the role of primary care in the prompt diagnosis and treatment of those in rural locations." Too late for GPs and their suffering patients.

IUCD

Inserting intrauterine contraceptive devices, also incorrectly but commonly called coils, was something I had always done. Having done an obstetrics job, I believed I knew my way around the uterus. In thirty-eight years, I had never had any trouble and had only used local anaesthetic on two occasions. If it hurt, I did not do it. The fashion of ladies seeing lady doctors was inexorable, so it was inevitable that one day, being a male Doctor – something I never thought I would have to apologise for – I would have to stop, but the pressure for IUCD insertion to be only done in clinics was unnecessary. I had attended many updating sessions over the years, and the questions from the attendees did not reveal the complexity of the procedure, it indicated their lack of experience and vested interest though the experience was very hard to come by. Insertion training of IUCDs had to be done through the Family Planning Association and meant that the doctor had to visit the clinic on around a dozen occasions. Why not let them do it all? As a result, many young doctors do not bother to learn the procedure.

As it happened, I was pretty slick at inserting IUCDs, and part of the credit must go to Timothy Spall when he played the part of Albert

Pierpoint, the last hangman in a TV play. Anyone who has read George Orwell's *A Hanging in Burma* will remember his observation that there was no-one present who actually wanted to go through with it. The decision had been judiciously made, and it was the law that the law and the condemned should be executed. It occurred to me that this situation shared similarities with the insertion of the IUCD. The patient and doctor had concluded that it would be a good idea, but when it came to the point of execution, neither party was terribly enthusiastic.

Albert Pierpoint, whose father and grandfather had been hangmen, was approached at the end of WW2 because there were a large number of war criminals to be despatched. He did not want to do it but concluded that if he did not do it, someone else would and nothing like as good! Therefore, he developed a technique to do the act in as humane a way as possible. The time between him entering the condemned person's cell and that person being dead was as short as possible because preparation had been completed beforehand, and the terrified thoughts in that person's mind would be over as quickly as he could manage. He said his PB (personal best) was seven seconds! I was very impressed with this and decided my technique would be equally quick and terror-free. I never used stirrups as I always thought them to be humiliating. Everything was kept ready before the procedure began. There was no unprofessional struggle to open the plastic containers with the IUCD – all of that would be ready. And by the time the lady asked if it was going well, I would tell her that it was done. I never had the time to measure my PB, but I do know that Albert was quicker!

FAMILY DIASPORA

I T IS NOT EASY TO be a real family doctor without families! In the early part of the new millennium, our practice manager had informed us that our list size was falling. The numbers were few, just three to four each quarter, but it was consistent and persistent. We were perplexed. We believed we were good doctors. We knew we ran a top-class practice, and our staff were superb. So, what was happening? I delved into the statistics. They showed that more people stayed than left. Most practices have a turnover of 5–10%, depending on the circumstances, but it was gratifying to note that more were staying than leaving. However, when I looked at the births and deaths, the problem was clear. We had far more deaths than births. The demographics were changing. The families that had moved in during the 1970s and 80s and had four to five persons to a household now had children who had grown up and left. So, these households were down to two persons. Also, the big houses were being replaced by flats for the elderly. And the youngsters could no longer afford to live in the town; they were moving to new towns attached to villages in the county. We were left with fewer families and more elderly folks. There is nothing wrong with this, of course. They all have to be looked after by someone, but the family doctor was no longer necessary or required. The new towns would attract their own family doctors but both the doctors and patients would start from scratch. I was lucky with the patients I had inherited, and if I started again, I would not work in Clayford or the new towns.

CHANGING WORKING PRACTICES

W^E WERE THE FIRST PORT of call for virtually any crisis – chest pain, stroke, renal colic, vertigo, whatever. We referred very little. I referred one patient in every twenty-two consultations to a hospital and my partners about one in twenty. When we were called out, we kept most things at home. One marker of what we did was the occasions when we administered a drug that came under the Dangerous Drugs Act, such as morphine or pethidine. These had to be recorded in a book we carried with us, and it acted as a record of some of the serious conditions we dealt with. So, in 1973 I gave, by injection, a DDA on fifteen occasions. In 1977, it was thirty-five occasions. Myocardial infarction was a common reason. This was usually followed by admission but not always. There was very little to be done that would be effective for a heart attack in the 70s. Once, a patient I had referred with unstable angina returned after he consulted with the specialist. *"What did he say?"* I asked. *"He told me to make a will,"* was the reply. He had a heart attack a few months later and died.

Biliary colic was another recurring reason as was abdominal pain and gastroenteritis. A surprising number of cases suffered from migraine, which could be terribly severe without the preventive measures we take today. Renal colic was a reliable one, especially in the dry hot summer of 1976 when you could almost say we had an epidemic of renal colic. The records show that apart from 1983 (goodness knows why), there was a steady decline in calls for such diseases. As time went on, chest pain and stroke cases went straight to the hospital, largely because the new treatments were effective; things could be done that made a difference. Even the diagnostic challenge of abdominal pains, which were so difficult to deal with in general practice, could be solved with a rapid CT scan. We were still busy but not with real emergencies. They began to bypass us, and in 2004, I gave my last injection of DDA drugs. Our ratio of visits to surgery consultations fell from 1:3 to 1:4 and so on until there were days with no visits.

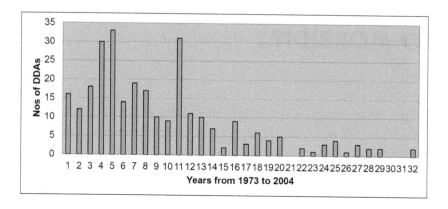

CO-MORBIDITY

C O-MORBIDITY MEANS HAVING MORE THAN one condition, which seems a bit unfair to the patient but is increasingly happening as we prolong life with more medical interventions and we alleviate illness without a cure. It is a problem for the specialist as they specialise in one discipline. The more the specialisation, the less they are inclined to stray into another speciality. Willis summed it all up in his book *The Paradox of Progress*. As the specialist (and this is not only in medicine) focuses more, they can discard information not appertaining to the speciality. Eventually, in this rarefied atmosphere, the specialist feels able to set rules and laws for others to obey. Unfortunately, in the real world, people don't confine themselves to artificial specialities and, thus, don't obey the laws. In the end, they have to fall back on a generalist, and the way things are going, the only generalist is the GP. As medical interventions become more complex, so do management problems.

This is not new, and I well remember such a complex problem of co-morbidity. The man in question had moved down here not too long ago and frequently called an ambulance, so I was asked to follow up. His wife, a heavy smoker, and his two adult daughters were unforgiving as I struggled with the problems.

In the end, I decided that some sort of counselling was required and asked the three of them to step outside onto the front doorstep out of earshot of the patient.

"How many," I asked, *"heart transplant patients do you think I have?"* There was a silence that became heavier when I asked them how many GPs in the country had patients who had had a heart transplant. I then asked them how many GPs in the country had a patient with a heart transplant which was in the process of rejection. So, I went on

with one question after another. He was undergoing heart failure. For good measure, he was also experiencing kidney failure. By the way, the transplant people had felt there was nothing further they could do, the cardiologists wanted the kidney side sorted before they acted, and the kidney people would not manage someone with heart failure. Additionally, he also had Type I diabetes and, diabolically, he had had shingles with severe post-herpetic neuralgia. It was the severity of the neuralgia that made him call an ambulance.

My last question was how many GPs in the country had a patient who had had a heart transplant, which was failing, and was experiencing heart failure and kidney failure and had Type 1 diabetes and uncontrollable neuralgia. I could have added, 'and had been kept at an arm's length by an assortment of specialists.' Clearly, there was only me, but even so, I was expected to pull a rabbit out of a hat. There was silence. I don't think our relationship changed, but I hope they had some insight into the challenge I was facing as a generalist. I added that their father was the bravest man I knew, which was a fact.

This was an extreme case then, but I doubt if it is now.

After retirement from the practice, I was drawn into locuming, at first against my will, but later, I realises that it was work without the responsibility – the icing on the cake. During that time, I worked in 'majors' at the local hospital. The contention was that GPs would, somehow, with their knowledge of the community, be able to prevent admissions. Alas, they were too far gone on arrival for that. Only on two occasions in six months was I able to prevent admission. Both were 'stroke' cases, but one was a total global amnesia case and the other was a Bell's palsy case. A typical problem was as follows: *"Can you see a head injury,"* I was asked. *"He has just fallen and bumped his head and may need a stitch."* Simple, except it is always a good idea to find out why the person fell. Was it neurological? Was it cardiac? Were they pushed! The man had a large bandage around his head and some blood was coming through. I asked him about the fall. There had been no loss of consciousness. He had not tripped. But then, he suggested it might be because he could not feel his feet. Could not feel his feet? Why? *"Oh, because of the neuropathy,"* he proffered. *"What neuropathy?"* I asked. *"The one secondary to the lymphoma,"* he replied. So now, he had a head injury, a lymphoma and peripheral neuropathy. *"Anything else?"* I quavered. *"The lymphoma seems to have upset things, and I have had clotting problems, so they put me on Warfarin two days ago."* So now, we have a man with a head injury, lymphoma and peripheral neuropathy, who was on blood thinners which was almost certainly not stabilised. And when the bandages came off, the little cut on his head turned out to be a macerated collection of lacerations and abrasions which took two of us two hours to sew up. This is co-morbidity, and it is a nightmare. Medical problems are now so complicated, even the simple ones!

2004

I N 2004, SOMETHING HAPPENED WHICH, on the face of it, was a godsend and certainly encouraged me to continue for another six years but also was probably the last nail in the coffin for the family doctor. A new contract was put forward, which offered to release us from our night and weekend responsibility for our patients for £6000 a year. We leapt at it, and the warnings of a few doctors who foresaw the death of our independence were ignored. £6000 sounds like a lot of money, but after tax, NI, superannuation, and the money we were paying deputies to do the 11 pm to 7 am shift, it was almost nothing at all. But having relinquished our 24-hour, 365-day responsibility, we had little power. GPs, having become 'clinic' doctors, steadily grew further away from their patients. Gordon Brown did one more wonderful thing. He increased our pension by 32%. He, in fact, said it would be 40%, and the BMA took him to court over it, won, and we got our 40%. As Aneurin Bevan said in 1947, our mouths were stuffed with gold.

"GPs work very little, are paid too much and have abrogated their responsibilities to secondary care. They get paid enough to work when they feel like it and only have responsibility to themselves." These were the words of a well-respected local consultant. He means them with bitterness, and I have to concur. Many young doctors, male and female, do not want the responsibility of partnership. They are happy to be "hired hands". A BMA paper in 2018 demonstrated that their lifetime earnings would be half of that of a partner, but this does not influence them. They had enough money and enjoyed their lifestyle. They had no ambition, but also, no yen to change anything. These young professionals are not very professional.

FINAL OBSERVATIONS

IT WOULDN'T BE ANY FUN if, after writing all this stuff, I was not allowed to give my unasked-for opinions about all and sundry. Over the years, I have formed several opinions, which were never repeated by anyone, but which I believe and know will be unrepeated and unsupported elsewhere.

I believe, after nearly five decades of observation, that spiteful women get early dementia. It gives me no pleasure to say this, but there is a sort of waspish woman who becomes demented early. I can't prove it, and a longitudinal study would take so long and be so subjective that I doubt it ever will. But it is my opinion.

Irritable bowel syndrome (IBS) and inflammatory bowel disease (IBD) can often be confused, especially in the early stages. Tests don't always give an answer, but I have always found my suspicions to be right. How do you tell the difference? Simple. Patients with IBS argue with you! That is why they get IBS. They are always at war with someone or something. IBS occurs in all countries of the world so diet cannot be the prime cause, although it may be an aggravating factor. It is stress-related. The question of why things that go on in the head influence what happens in the bowel is an interesting one, but it has something to do with the fact that living organisms had bowels before they had brains, and the brain borrowed some of the neurological pathways.

The more you talk about ethical problems, the more complicated they become. There is no limit as to how complicated human beings can make anything. This can be a problem in a ten-minute consultation! In our current world of drugs, gender dysphoria, diversification, medical advances, genetic manipulation, paedophilia, grooming and the danger of hurting someone's feelings, I accept that ethical problems in medicine are more complicated than they ever were. The most common issue in my day was prescribing a contraceptive pill to underaged girls. Nowadays, it is not a problem, but for a family doctor who had to consider the family as well as the patient, it was. But if a girl was having regular sex with a boy of her own age, she needed contraception. Full stop. It was right to ask what the girl's mother or father might think. They used to have an interest in their children in the good old days! Sometimes, the girls would be adamant that they did not want their parents to know and were dismayed when I told them that all mothers search their daughter's handbags, belongings, secret places, etc. I also told them that if they ever did become pregnant, their mother would always stand by them. Not always the father. But in the end, the mother always did.

The thing that is going to get you is something that you never thought of. This is not such a brilliant thing to say because, in many cases, if you had thought about it, you would have avoided it. This was a statement I usually trotted out to hypochondriacs. Genuine hypochondriacs are mercifully few, but we all had some. One unfortunate lady had had just about every part of her body scanned and investigated despite my desperate attempts at being a gatekeeper. She was unfortunate because her mother had died in the passenger seat while she had been driving, so she always wondered whether it was her bad driving that had delivered the final coup. One day, I counselled her as we stumbled towards another investigation, *"The thing that is going to get you is something you would not have thought of."* *"I know,"* she said, *"that is why I think of everything!"* Some, you just can't win!

LOOKING BACK

WHEN I STARTED IN GENERAL practice, our week, included Saturday mornings and nights and weekends on a rota. I did that for nineteen years and then, mercifully, another fifteen without the 11 pm to 7 am shift. Who thought that this was a reasonable way of working? The phone went through to the house and a call in the night nearly always meant getting out of bed, driving to a sick patient and not returning for an hour, often longer. There was always another day to work and no guarantee that there would not be another night call before that day's work began. This was not a good way to induce sleep. I would venture that it was impossible for anyone to look happy all the time under those circumstances. And yet, we did it, mainly because it was considered normal. The modern GP does not work nights and weekends and rarely does a full week's work. We had an afternoon off to balance the night and weekend work. The modern GP does not do nights and weekends but still has an afternoon or a day off or more.

So, why are they so unhappy? After seventeen years of appraising doctors and delving into their working practices, I can honestly say that I do not entirely know. There must surely be a host of reasons, including the type of person that becomes a doctor. For the general public, being a doctor is a vocation, but in reality, for many doctors, it is an intellectual exercise and a good way of earning a decent living. There is no vocation and no inspiration. For many lady doctors, it is a good option to get a profession with the flexibility to bring up their children. I understand it, but it will not last a lifetime.

Undoubtedly, one stressful factor is the obligation of 'niceness'. Young doctors are now chosen because they are 'nice' people. The culture of niceness continues throughout their career. The target, when

I trained, was to be good. If you were nice as well, it was a bonus. But as Roger Neighbour said, *"Nobody dies if their doctor is rude or isn't nice to them. People die if you miss their burst appendix. So, the most important is clinical safety, but beyond that, it's communication."* But our clinical governance-based medicine and the threat of vexatious complaints means that while the target was to be good first and nice second, the target now is to be nice always and follow guidelines. Not following guidelines is worse than getting things wrong.

Vexatious complaints are one of the most dispiriting things for doctors. Many complaints are entirely justifiable; for instance, if you miss detecting diabetes, having never done a blood test or tested the urine. But a vexatious complaint is one where there is no medical issue. You may have been perceived to have been rude or had not noticed a woman's children or had hurt their feelings. The complainant has no come back on their complaint. They risk nothing. They can accuse the doctor of anything they like, and the doctor will always be on the back foot. NHS England, the GMC, will investigate these complaints as though they are potentially genuinely serious. The defence bodies, who make their livelihood from these issues, insist that everything is reported to them and sent to them, which often gives credence to the most trivial patient dissatisfaction. This also gives credence to the patient who, possibly for the only time in their life, is now in a position of importance. In my many years of appraising GPs, many of these vexatious, trivial and outrageous complaints have amazed me. Yes, they are dispiriting indeed.

Our target-based culture has to be blamed. Working to meet targets – government targets and not patient needs – inevitably means failure. It is a huge challenge to achieve all the targets all of the time. Some doctors do feel a sense of worthlessness as a result.

There was another change, which may be the same reason that I gave up locuming seven years post retirement from the practice. It was great fun at first, but after a while, it was the patients who changed. In my practice with personal lists for thirty-eight years, there was always the incentive to do one's best for the patient, and they reciprocated this, with their families, by caring for the doctor. There was positive feedback, and this sustained the incentive to do one's best. I locumed in several different areas in the county. In one, a deprived area, people had settled there because of low rents. They did not want to be there once they became aware of the drug and alcohol problems that were rife but had no way of getting out. They were depressed, yes, but it was the sense of hopelessness that was so dispiriting. In another area in the centre of the town, about a third of the people I saw were immigrants, mainly from Southern Europe and the Eurozone. They too did not want to be there. Why would anyone from southern Spain want to work in a Bournemouth Hotel? The answer is unemployment in the home country. The effect of the Euro had produced massive youth unemployment in Southern Europe, which was up to 30–50% in some places. It was a huge betrayal to the generation by the EU, which was made merely bearable by allowing them to do low paid jobs in the UK. The title 'unskilled migrants' is usually quite wrong in my experience. These were skilled migrants doing low paid, unskilled jobs. They too didn't want to be there and were depressed. These were the people I saw also with their own sense of hopelessness.

The third group of unfortunates is the people in nursing homes. One imagines that when the time comes, one's loved one, or even oneself, will enter a cosy home to be cared for in the twilight years. There's no doubt this happens, but there is another side to it. Modern medicine can maintain a life beyond what is reasonable, sensible or humane. The state we allow people to reach so that the only thing they are aware of is discomfort and pain is pitiful.

All in all, I found diminishing pleasure in caring for these people, and I imagine it is the same for the modern GP. The characters I looked after were, well – as the anecdotes about the patients above demonstrate – characters. However quirky, awkward and annoying they were, they were memorable. They all had a place in society like Tom Shearing, the Raven, who roamed East Dorset on his bike. With many of our patients now, one asks oneself what their place is. I am sure they want one.

So, the old family doctor, who was always there, faded away. They faded because the medical practice changed, the doctors wanting a life and variety changed, and the concept of the family changed. I understand all this, and I am not advocating what we had but just commenting on it. Usually, at this stage, someone would call me a dinosaur. Apart from the fact that I embraced every innovation I could, including running the practice website and some that others could not see, I would make this observation. The dinosaurs, with hundreds of species, dominated the world for millions of years and were eventually destroyed by the planet. Homo sapiens, just one species, in a hundred thousand years, is destroying the planet. The world at present is undoubtedly a lot worse than the one I lived in. We all look back to a golden time, but it is mainly because we were young. You can't beat youth. Notwithstanding, I am so glad I am not a GP today. What will they have to look back on?

FINALLY – THE FLIP SIDE

WITHIN OUR FAMILIES, WE HAVE heartache and tragedy – some families more than others. We bear them, and as long as they are not overwhelming, we cope. In family practice, the heartache and tragedy can be overwhelming. One remembers those who did not die well, those with appalling death sentences, like motor neurone disease, the cot deaths and the sudden deaths. I remember a lovely couple who were at home one evening – he was watching TV and she was doing the ironing – when they heard a thump upstairs and found their twenty-one-year-old daughter dead on the floor. There were no explainable factors. Post-mortem explained nothing. Parts of the girl's heart were sent to learned pathologists around the country but no explanation for this dreadful event was ever found. Decades later, I saw this couple walking the streets hand in hand. Their only child was taken for no fathomable reason. As the decades went by, there was no road, lane or street in Clayford that I could not relate to some awful happening. On some roads, it was every house. I pass the place where old Sam hanged himself from the great apple tree. On another road is the drive where the young man, I never knew him, gassed himself in the car from the exhaust. That was bad enough, but the poignant part of the memory is the faithful black Labrador that lay next to him, partners in life and death. And so, it goes on. This is why my trips to the town I worked in for so long are brief and infrequent.

Even so, as Don Berwick put it in his John Hunt lecture while talking about the influence of his father, *"It is a privilege (for the Family Doctor) to enter the dark and tender places of people's minds."* But it took its toll.

Lightning Source UK Ltd.
Milton Keynes UK
UKHW010237231220
375546UK00012B/363